Date

CRAFTING CHARACTER
THE ARCHITECTURAL PRACTICE OF CHYBIK + KRISTOF

ISBN: 978-94-92311-60-3

CHYBIK + KRISTOF + AARON BETSKY =
FOREWORD

Founded a little over a decade ago in the city in which the principals still work and live, Chybik + Kristof (CHK) is a firm with projects around the Czech Republic and beyond. While they are part of a generation of designers shaped by conditions, whether they are economic or cultural, that are global in their definition and character, they also seek to build on the strengths of what they recognise as local traditions, which include the strong vein of Czech Functionalism that dotted their city with modernist structures in the intra-War era.

Their particular strength, although it is one they do not emphasise themselves, is their ability to use their European position and training, while also developing and extending that functionalism and the coherence and flexibility that the countries that were formerly part of the Austro-Hungarian Empire exhibit in their grid of flats and Beaux-Arts monuments growing out of the landscape-specific forms of medieval towns. Combining the best of Bata, the company that commissioned a whole town of Functionalist structures, with the reserve of an older Brno and the softly undulating fields, dotted with hills and river, that mark Moravia, they are thus at their best when they translate what they have learned living there into a part of the global flow of forms and spaces in which they grew up. 'We seek to create not stand-alone sculptures,' says Kristof, 'but buildings that open up their context.'

The firm was founded by Ondřej Chybík and Michal Krištof when they were still students at the Brno University of Technology. Chybík's father, though an engineer and not an architect, was Dean of the Architecture School, giving the son entree to a wide social and technical network. Krištof came to the School from Slovakia, attracted to the University's strong reputation. While Chybík also studied at the Technical Universities of Graz and Zurich (ETH), apprenticing at the Viennese firm PPAG, Krištof used the EU's Erasmus Program to study at the Catholic University of Leuven's Academy of Sint-Lucas in Ghent, Belgium, and also worked for Bjarke Ingel's firm, BIG, in Copenhagen. Their origins within what used to be Czechoslovakia and their experiences in western Europe in themselves mark them as children of the new reality that has emerged in the old 'Middle Europe' this century.

They describe an atmosphere at the University of Technology in which they were able to shape debates and enter competitions in a manner that opened the view from their small, but sophisticated provincial capital to a much larger world that they were then able to inhabit in their exchange programs and positions. Yet at the same time they felt deeply shaped by the landscape in which they grew up, and see themselves as making projects out of that experience – in some cases quite literally, as in the self-initiated transformation of Brno's Communist-era bus station.

To be specific, the strong emphasis on technology (which Chybík also gained at home), along with the building programmes in which the Communist regime engaged in the 1970s and 1980s to anchor and house the communal society they went back to building after the Prague Spring of 1968, created a base of structures that were innovative and expressive in how they were built, that emphasised their public nature and a need for collective expression, and that sought to distinguish themselves from the heritage in which they appeared. What Chybík and Krištof have sought to do is not only to build on what by now is part of their heritage, but also to recapture the other strains present in Brno and Middle Europe in general, and to then streamline and open them up into architecture that exploits the generic, mass produced and data- and regulation-driven building blocks of construction anywhere in the world.

This method of working is nowhere clearer than in the successions of projects they have designed for Koma, a manufacturer of steel armatures covered in a flexible array of materials that can serve as temporary housing, kiosks or building blocks for larger structures. While they were still in school, the principals won a competition to showcase the company's approach to modular construction through the design of a small housing project, and have since completed several projects that now make up almost all of the public and administrative side of Koma's headquarters in Vizovice, a small town down-valley from the Bata city of Zlin.

The company is itself the outgrowth of the Eastern Bloc's drive toward standardised production that would make spaces and amenities available to the masses. As a privatised company, it has continued to focus on such provisions through its production of emergency facilities, while also developing methods that allow the simple steel frame to form the basis for more elaborate and upmarket buildings. Chybik + Kristof have followed them in this movement, moving from the design of the kiosk to the creation of a company canteen to the adaption of a structure they designed as the Czech Pavilion at the Milan International Expo in 2015 as an office building, to the most experimental of the structures on the small campus, a smushing together of pavilions that serve as a showcase for the possibilities of Koma's modular technology.

The complex shows Chybik + Kristof's work at its simplest and most reductive. The canteen in particular is an essay in reserved form. By leaving the structural grid on the inside of the building, capping the cages on the top and bottom with strong bands of dark-coloured metal, and then wrapping the horizontal surfaces completely with glass (including where they cover the back of the kitchen wall), they turned Koma's grids into a floating plane. That appearance of a modernist pavilion is made even stronger by the manner

The studio's first completed project, Modular Cafeteria, 2013, Vizovice

in which they have floated it over protruding boxes covered with metal mesh, which hide building's ancillary service, but also connect it to the strong datum of a one-storey base that unifies the campus.

The office building is much larger and more refined, both in its material and in its proportions. It was originally built as the Czech Pavilion for the World Expo in Milan in 2015 and then moved to the site afterwards. Here two floors of offices, surmounted by an outdoor terrace, hover over a base that is again visually suppressed. The much larger bulk takes on a presence of its own, further removed in appearance from the canteen not only by its shape and size, but also because the architects covered the façade with thin white slats – like almost all the materials visible here fabricated in the factory hall behind these structures – leaving the windows to ghost the façade with their rhythm. A refined use of details that is both matter-of-fact, with plates and structural members abutting each other with little to no transition, and carefully considered in how each element is emphasised and held away from each other, fine-tunes the aesthetic of this and most of Chybik + Kristof's buildings. There is little signing of Koma's system, but that is exactly the point: both the client and the architect wanted to emphasise the ability of the simplest and most repetitive technology, produced with local craft, to serve the purpose of housing and representing functions in a manner that is almost neutral, and yet expressive of exactly that minimalism.

The most daring and spatially interesting of the structures is what Koma terms its Modular Research Centre. Here Chybik + Kristof assembled the steel cages not into solid forms, but into a hexagonal grouping, stretching the system as far as they could. Inside what appears to be an undulating object fronted by more metal mesh and glass are the basic frames, but they now serve as structure between the spaces: the structure has become a block, housing such functions as a small kitchen and bathrooms. These objects are covered in a version of the metal panels that appear all over the campus, but here they are both tighter and more polished. What gives the building its strong character, beyond the off-kilter configuration, are the hexagonal cones that surmount each of the spaces and terminate in a skylight. As tall as the habitable rooms, they give the pavilion a sense of grandeur.

Within these grids, sleek walls, and grand gestures, the space flows past white-painted furniture Chybik + Kristof designed to reflect in miniature Koma's cubes. Where privacy is needed, the architects devised a system of undulating rails from which they suspended curtains made out of the durable and affordable fabric used by caterers. Taken together, these design elements create a luminous and sensuous environment that is deeply rooted in fabrication and standardisation, but finds moments of specificity, variation and elegance within and out of that system. The project sums up Chybik + Kristof's work with Koma to this point, although they will continue to work with them as the company both expands its reach and refines its systems.

Such a minimal and systems-based approach is on display in the other most notable of Chybik + Kristof's early commissions, a small furniture showroom on a busy commercial street on Brno's periphery. It is actually a renovation of what had been one of the many non-descript and cheaply built commercial structures that line an arterial road giving access to one of the neighbourhoods of plattenbau flats built in the 1970s and 1980s. Moreover, the client, a furniture company based in Prague, leased the space for only 5 years, although they have since extended their occupation.

The architects' solution was to use what is on sale inside as a sign and exterior system rolled into one. They covered the façades facing the public with the plastic chair shells that are at the core of what the company sells. The architects chose black examples and lined them up in a staggered pattern, creating a crenelated cornice and base that suggests the arrangement is infinite. It also feathers the building into the sky and ground, dematerialising the box and making the structure part of the array of signs that dominate this commercial strip. The grid of chair shells gives way to a few windows into offices, but otherwise the building has become a field rather than an object. With a scale that is both definite when you come close and recognise the shells for what they are, and that dissolves into pixelation as you cruise past on the highway, the structure manages to move from the modern urban to the specific with one bit of architecture.

The most extreme version of this focus on infinite structures made specific is Chybik + Kristof's renovation of the Brno Central Bus Station. Once the largest such facility in the Czech Republic, it was an object lesson in structural innovation the two partners had to study in school because its three-way truss supported the weight of several dozen buses that parked on its roof before pulling into their covered stalls below to pick up passengers. Chybík got to know the site well when he spent many an hour waiting for transportation to see his then-girlfriend, and conceived the idea that the space should be a civic anchor, rather than a neglected facility. The project to make that possible was self-directed, with the architects approaching the new owner once the depot was privatised, and finally convincing them to restore the existing building. It shows their and their generation's ability to fully appreciate a past that their parents did not always think of kindly.

Here Chybik + Kristof's architecture consists first and foremost in acts that are not necessarily structural, such as lighting and simply cleaning the building so that its beauty and innovation are revealed. What they then added was a place to wait for buses, buy tickets and use toilets, all of which they housed in a ribbon structure at the building's front. A proposed connection to the shopping mall across the street, which in turn connects through Brno's main train station to the town's historic core, has yet to be constructed. Even so, with this simple and humble act of renovation and addition, the architects have here made an essential contribution to Brno's architecture scene.

Czech Pavilion at Expo 2015, completed, 2015, Milan

The project also ties their work directly to the scene in which most of their teachers and parents were trained and worked. While both Krištof and Chybík cite what they feel is their direct connection to the work of Adolf Loos (who was born in Brno) above all others, noting his ability to open up and abstract the Austro-Hungarian traditions that shaped most of Brno and the Czech Republic's other cities, as well as to local heroes such as Ernst Wiesner, Bohuslav Fuchs and Jaroslav Josef Polívka, who streamlined and modernised that same history, the perhaps unconscious connection to the period of the post-Prague Spring of 1968 seems particularly strong to this outside observer. In addition, of course the presence of Ludwig Mies van der Rohe's Tugendhat House in Brno emanated an aura of modernism beyond the local.

The concentration on the making of a civic architecture, or one that contributes to the civic sphere even when it is private; the confidence in making large gestures; and the love of systems expressed in exposed structure, all tie into the period when architects such as Vera and Vladimir Machonins, Jan Sramek, Jan Bocan, Ivan Ruller and Milan Rejchl were part of a European-wide program of social building. This was a period when facilities for the people, from new train and bus stations to sports halls, museums, civic centres and recreational centres such as ski resorts, were built from Moscow to the Alps. Their aim was to build a new world that would benefit the population in general in a way that represented what the Dutch, for instance, called the 'makeable' or 'shapeable' community.

Urban Infill Lofts, completed, 2019, Brno

That impulse lives on in the design Chybik + Kristof have done in and in front of the St. Thomas Monastery where Georg Mendel did his work on grafting in the 19th century. The greenhouse in which the scientist monk laboured is long gone, but the architects have now created a new glass structure that evokes, without copying, the old building. They also once again used their technique of abstracting and deforming a system, in this case the rhythm of metal and glass that structures a shed with a linear proportion and a gabled roof. Here they distorted the angle of the peaked structure to present an almost rhetorical façade that also tilts towards the sun, offering an image of science and clarity to visitors coming into the complex. Inside, the building is an open volume that can be used for events, whether social or educational. The proportions of each of the windows and the bays in which they fit are broader and more horizontal than you would expect in a greenhouse, giving the simple building a stretch while also opening to the courtyard and surrounding historic buildings. In addition, shades can roll down to protect the interior from the sun, turning what is an almost completely transparent and light object into a solid one that takes its place among the stucco-covered convent structures around it.

In the square in front of the monastery, Chybik + Kristof, together with Michal Palascak and Zdenek Sendler, are working to transform a welter of buses, cars and pedestrians into an ordered square. Using minimal means, including paving patterns, lighting poles, benches and a few shelters, they are marking and measuring this public territory so that it becomes a place. As in their object buildings, they have made sure not to see the square as a separate entity with a specific fabric, but rather have made it into an intensification and articulation of the surrounding streets, sidewalks and other elements of the civic continuum.

The design where Chybik + Kristof's approach to architecture comes together most clearly so far is in the Lahofer Winery they designed in the middle of the Moravian countryside near the town of Znojmo, about an hour from Brno. Here they were able to translate their interest in system and form into housing for what is both a productive and a consumptive environment. This gives the building a mandate to be regular, efficient and expandable, but also means it needs to create a dramatic and attractive space for wine tasting and buying.

Here the system – or rather, systems – start with the land itself and how humans have transformed it. A curved roof dominates the tasting and vending room, rising out of the rolling hills to become a human-made version of its site. Cutting through that wave and turning into the structural system of the factory sheds behind is a line of concrete columns. These precisely follow the rows of vines growing the grapes that are the reason for the building to exist. The vertical elements support what appears from the vineyard to be a flat roof with glass rises between them, so that the pavilion invites the landscape inside. Only from an angle does it become obvious that the eaves are just the beginning of the curve, whose rise is supported in the tasting room's interior by rows of concrete arches that turn the interior into an evocation of the often underground caves that house the more traditional vineyard venues of the region. That wave then subsides at an angle to support an outdoor amphitheatre where grid and landscape come together and guests can enjoy outdoor concerts.

Lahofer's major public space is grand. It exhibits the linearity of which Chybik + Kristof are so fond, but opens it up into a rhythm of bays that breaks down its scale and connects from the sweeping view to the vineyard to the dense wall of storage opposite, behind which a private tasting room is visible from one window. It is by far the grandest space these architects have designed to date, and the manner in which it is anchored, both in the landscape and by the simple concrete structures behind whose panels are filled in with wood continuing the material of the wine barrels, roots the experience even more strongly in its program.

The follow-up to this building is an interior renovation for a tasting room the architects designed in a nearby town. They left the actual place where you sample wines almost untouched, and worked hard to renovate much of the existing spaces. In the front section, they created a condensed, but also freer stack of boxes reminiscent of their earlier work to spiral here through the adjacent space and create a cafe and a bar. The dark wood panels of the platforms on which groups of people can sit have the effect of putting the patrons on stage along with the architecture. This is the most expressive structure Chybik + Kristof have designed, and shows a mastery of spatial relations that they are now developing in more complex buildings. Their design for the Czech Forestry Agency, outside of Prague, is promising in that respect. Splaying out from a central core, it offers a large variety of spaces the architects have derived from a simple structural and spatial module formed, of course, by timber elements. However, if the buildings described above are the most striking Chybik + Kristof have designed so far (in addition to several competition entries that, though dramatic, cannot be judged in their unrealised state), the financial, if not the philosophical core of the practice, has been the design of housing. And, while they have recently started working on commissions for large private homes, that practice has in turn focused on the design and building of multi-unit structures in urban contexts, both in Brno and in Prague.

In this work, the architects have concentrated on designing structures whose simplicity and clarity both contributes to their surroundings and provides well-organised living spaces. The small building they designed on a street where a fragment of the old Habsburg grid confronts now open fields that will soon be developed stands as a prototype – albeit a somewhat unusual one – for the larger projects they have designed since then. Restricted in the amount of floors they were allowed to build in this gap between existing and planned apartment buildings, they discovered that they had some freedom to extend their building's height by creating double-storey living units on the top levels. This, in turn, gave them a chance to create a bit of space and drama within the apartments, while also boosting the building's ability to stand as a corner marker slightly above its neighbours. In this manner, they recaptured the Austro-Hungarian tradition of marking intersections with such small towers and turrets. They then cut the corner below to

shelter the entrance, allowed the sidewalk to pass by, and emphasised the raised piece as a volume emerging out of the adjacent street façades.

Chybik + Kristof have worked hard in their other apartment buildings to provide this kind of variety and drama in what is of necessity a system of repetitive elements that must be produced at a low cost. Although most of their efforts until recently have been relatively small, several recent projects are increasing their scales of operation. The first of these is the Francouzska (or, as it is now called, Municipal Affordable) Housing project in Brno. This was a project commissioned by the city, so that they were free to experiment and develop new modes of communal living. Also, here the firm has the chance not only to work at scale, and to create a neighbourhood into itself, but also to pursue a tectonic strategy that the largely stucco-covered context of this and most Czech cities precludes.

Consisting of 6 structures that together house 90 units organised around interior courtyards and alleys, the Francouzska project presents itself as a refined version of the kind of work Chybik + Kristof did for Koma. Clad in corrugated metal (at least at the current design stage) and fronted by balconies supported by thin metal posts, the whole district will be considerably lighter and more open than most of its older surroundings. Covered walkways will connect many of the structures to small stores and cafes.

Even within the structures themselves, the architects have worked to open up what structures usually marked by: their closed, cellular nature. They did so mainly by taking a tactic that has become central to how architects wrest spatial effects out of tightly packed commercial and cultural buildings, namely to concentrate all their efforts on open stairways that turn into atria, and apply it to housing. The over-scaled, but simply detailed and mainly translucent stair halls have equally large landings that in some cases extend up several storeys. Chybik + Kristof envision these as places of gathering or chance encounters – of children playing, teens studying and older people having a conversation. It is a remarkably romantic vision that brings together a modern aesthetic with a socialist or social democratic utopia of community.

Vila Park Olomouc, ongoing, 2015–2024, Olomouc

An even larger development is the Sugar Factory on the outskirts of Prague. The community will eventually consist of close to eight hundred apartments and almost 7000 m² of public space stretched out along the banks of the Vitava River. The plan is to maintain and restore parts of the ruins of the old factory that gives the project its name, but also to develop and adjust the form of residential development that has taken place since its demise: low-rise apartment buildings that dot the higher reaches of the bank.

Chybik + Kristof have taken great pains here to reuse and recycle what they can, including working with a new composite concrete made of recycled bricks and aggregates. They also see the public space as encompassing not only formal areas, but also restored riparian reserves and swales that will help put water from both rain and the river to good use. The new buildings will rise in will rise framed and tinted a reddish colour both to distinguish them from the white-coloured older apartments, and to blend them into the earth hues of the surroundings. The grids here will be large and insistent, as Chybik + Kristof have sculpted them with beveled edges and continued them both down to the ground as colonnades and up into the sky as friezes. Proportioned to emphasise their height, these towers are a humble version of Le Corbusier's vision of high-rises in a park setting for both the business elite at the core of the development's audience and the larger audience it seeks to attract.

Chybik + Kristof are now looking beyond both the projects that allowed their office to grow, designing structures such as an ice hockey arena and the new home for the Czech Forestry Agency, and beyond their borders. They believe that the methods they have developed out of the culture in which they were trained – both the local one, steeped in a combination of traditional, modernist and Communist-brutalist modes of building – and the international one, with its ability to put computers to work to rationalise, abstract and open this heritage, will give them the ability to compete at a global scale. They certainly are one of the most ambitious, most accomplished, and most promising firms to come out of both the pan-European embrace of the reductive kind of modernism pioneered by firms such as the Office for Metropolitan Architecture (OMA) and the particular situation of those countries that remained isolated by half a century of Communist rule – and centuries of domination by other countries and cultures before that – and it will be worth seeing how they modulate their gridded aesthetic and open structures as their sites expand.

Aaron Betsky

Waltrovka residential complex, together with ADR and Martin Rudiš, completed, 2019, Prague

CHYBIK + KRISTOF + TEAM = CONTEXT

In no discipline is context more important than in architecture. When trying to introduce improvements or an entirely new structure to a specific site, it's critical for practitioners to fully engage not only with environmental constraints but also address the different histories and understand contemporary needs. The ultimate aim, as demonstrated in the Lahofer Winery project, is to introduce new functions that can complement all three. There's nothing better than a new building that has settled into the place from which it draws inspiration and that seems to have always been there. This approach stands in contrast to International Style Modernism, which imposed a more standardised, non-contextual vision. This chapter of Crafting Character explores Chybik + Kristof's ability to utilise context as a canvas on which to realise holistic designs that not only fit into their surroundings but also respond to cultural, social and environmental factors.

CHYBIK + KRISTOF + TEAM + VINARSTVI LAHOFER + DOBSICE, CZ = **LAHOFER WINERY**

Year: 2015–2020
Type: mixed-use, civic, offices, production
Size: 3842 m²
Investment: EUR 6,000,000
Status: completed

Grapevine is

n my veins.

I stand i

heir rhythm

and look up to

my surroundings.

Sliding in the

andscape

I'm echoing

he tradition.

Aligned with

ny archetype

I reflec

his place.

Inspired by the ric

soil I stand on...

...I'm grounded

n my purpose.

Embedded in the Moravian uplands, my undulating roofline perches above lush vineyards that extend as far as the eye can see. Nestled in the curvilinear recesses of this setting's topography, my arched windows evoke the many wine vaults that have historically characterised this soil-rich region. Naturally, my gambrel features a hill-like viewing platform and cascading amphitheatre that perfectly frames sweeping views of this expanse landscape while forming a seamless connection with the ground. It's almost as if I've always been here or at least should have been. Though new to this site, my design – developed from 2015 to 2020 – corresponds to existing conditions, yet actively confronts the site's dependencies and idiosyncrasies.

As Lahofer Winery's combined production facility, administrative offices and visitor centre – complete with a spacious tasting room that doubles as a community hub – I take on different roles. I do so without overpowering my surroundings. I'm well-contained and embody the practical architectural and viticulture tradition of this terrain. With enclosed halls defined by frames of cast-concrete beams, my imprint has a minimal impact on otherwise fertile land. Each was individually engineered to ensure that my floorplate could navigate the nuanced angles of the gentle slope I sit upon. If that weren't enough, they were painstakingly proportioned to reflect the space between the vine rows outside. Still, these elements allow me to achieve visual symmetry. Custom floor-to-ceiling glass windows make my presence even less intrusive. No stone has been left unturned.

In fact, the contemporary Czech artist Patrik Hábl has transformed my ceilings with a mural that depicts the geological evolution of the location using sparse strokes of granite grey, earthy red and terroir beige. Znojmo, the place where I am currently situated, has a tumultuous history. The subsequent invasions and influences over the centuries have mirrored gradual changes in grapevine-dependent soil composition. Hábl's site-specific artwork, *Layers*, captures this transformation, resembling an in-depth colour study, a surveyed map of past and present.

I could have been your run-of-the-mill modular kit-out sourced from a catalogue and unceremoniously plopped on a flattened, rectilinear plot of land; objectified like so many other cookie-cutter facilities. It could have been me, placed on this very site with little consideration but it wasn't. I stand out from the rest but not in a fussy way. I'm not an extravagant expression of an architect's singular vision. My form and function directly reference the site I occupy and the bespoke needs of the everyday users that enter my confines.

I negotiate between contemporary requirements, the human and ecological history of the surroundings and attempt to do so with a light touch. It's less about appeasement and more about achieving compromise and mutual respect through astute considerations of my intricate situation. My organic contours are far more reflective of my daily operations than they might seem. An exposed rib structure towers just high enough to keep my sizable barrique cellars temperate.

Am I visually succinct? Is my role easily decipherable to those passing by or those already planning to experience what I have to offer? Much like the artwork that adorns my ceiling, can these visitors engage with my history, can they sense how I've assimilated into my new surroundings, or does my performance make it all seem so effortless? Only time will tell.

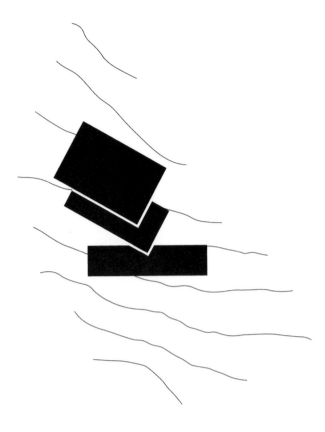

The position of the building reacts to the terrain

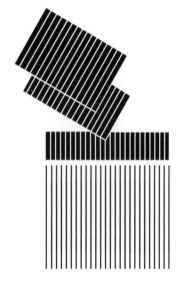

Continuity of the vineyards as a rhythm of the structure

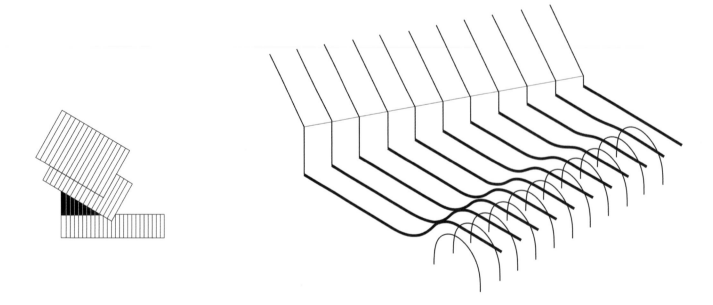

The amphitheatre is connecting two parts of the building

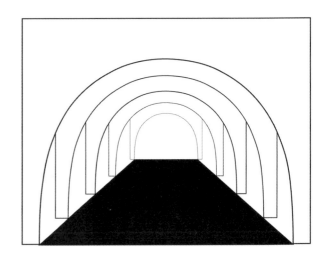

The interior reflects the archetypal shape of the region's wine cellars

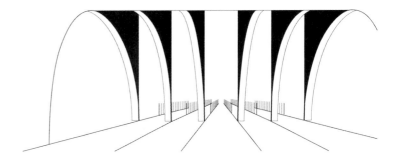

The design allows an unobstructed view toward the vineyards

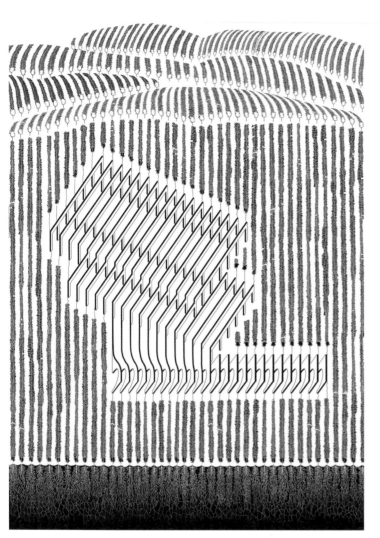
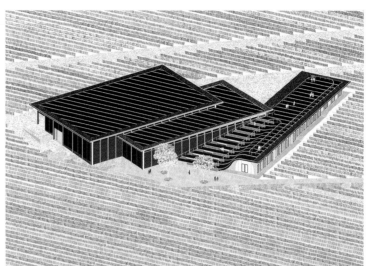
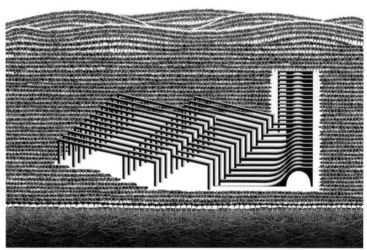

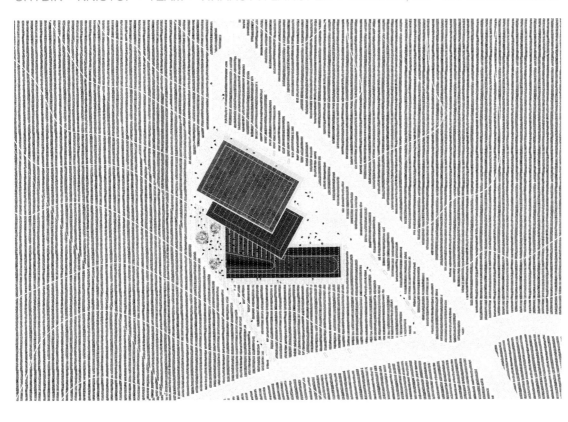

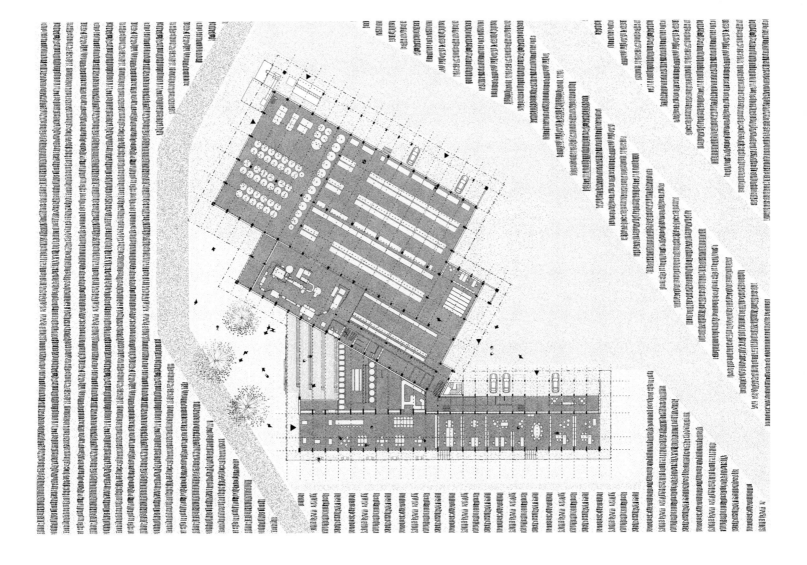

CHYBIK + KRISTOF + TEAM = ADAPTIVE REUSE

Should architecture still be so concerned with the construction of new buildings or in finding ingenious ways of re-activating the abundant inventory of underutilised structures that already define our surroundings? Responding to our changing requirements, the built environment is in constant flux.
As economic and cultural priorities shift, so does the function of space. To effectively reconfigure a building's purpose, architects need to embrace both old and new. Chybik + Kristof frequently employs adaptive reuse as a resourceful, creative, and forward-looking approach that encompasses not only waste reduction and the curbing of CO_2 emissions, but also embraces a holistic interplay of references, aesthetics, programming and usage that reflects the essence of the location. As demonstrated in the House of Wine, Gallery of Furniture, Perla Gallery and Broadway Adaptive Reuse projects, conversion and revitalisation are essential parts of shaping our world going forward. However, such interventions rarely follow a standardised rubric. Each endeavour must negotiate between historical relevance and contemporary demands on its own terms. The answers are not always obvious when trying to infuse an age-old structure with new purpose. Nevertheless, architects should increasingly focus their thinking on uncovering the potential of disused infrastructures. This chapter of Crafting Character investigates Chybik + Kristof's prowess in transformation and adaptive reuse: giving new life to existing structures by implementing various strategies, all while preserving the past.

⚓ CHYBIK + KRISTOF + TEAM + VINARSTVI LAHOFER + ZNOJMO, CZ = **HOUSE OF WINE**

Year: 2017–2019
Type: retail, transformation, interior
Size: 550 m²
Investment: EUR 550,000
Status: completed

Within m

y histories

I invite you

o explore

different lay

s of my story

it's full o

iances.

I'm a pa

mpsest.

Gazing out from my

...ew standpoint...

...I reflect o

he past.

Preservation is a complex undertaking. Structures like my 19th-century-brewery and adjacent 1970s technical space were not created equal. I incorporate a network of historical and contemporary buildings within the heart of Znojmo, Czech Republic. Ensuring the success of my transformation and identifying which of my characteristics were worth refreshing was determined by negotiating different, at times conflicting, expectations. As a palimpsest, I still maintain traces of my previous function but answer to the public's changing needs. Part of my restoration was understanding what could be considered as historically significant and what couldn't. It was also about seeing where major improvements could be made to ensure that it could meet contemporary standards and my owner's requirements. Sometimes, renovations are too intrusive and other times, too limited. What's clear is that not everything old is precious and merits being saved.

Untraditionally, my architects made the bold decision to forsake my more recent addition and hold on to my original structure by enhancing the elements that best communicate a clear narrative. While the former space underwent a surgical conversion – introducing a new matrix of volumes that serve multiple functions, the latter was treated with a more conventional form of restoration.

By applying a meticulous process, my architects discovered that if something isn't broken, it doesn't need to be fixed. Of course, they introduced upgrades that now help me function smoothly and answer present-day demands. Both strategies were equally valid and demonstrated how I could come to life again in 2019 thanks to the architects' prowess in effectively combining disparate yet equally innovative restoration practices.

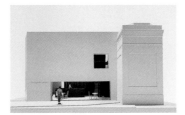

Throughout my setting, I contain a complex clarity of architectural symbolism that reflects my context: cave, cellar, cathedral and rock formation motifs. These are elements that could easily be perceived as contrived, gimmicky or out of date but the studio impressively distilled and masterfully interpreted these historical references as useful attributes. My architects imbued one of the bars with a stacked, curvilinear wooden balcony insert. This insert incorporated various spaces to sit and enjoy wine.

For me, it's about blending into my surroundings.
The architects positioned a number of asymmetrical
windows throughout my exterior so that those tasting wine
could also look out at the historical architecture that defines
Znojmo. They added cuts and inserted massing that open
up previous closed-off apertures to better frame a nearby
valley and striking church-top hill.

Am I an extrovert or an introvert?

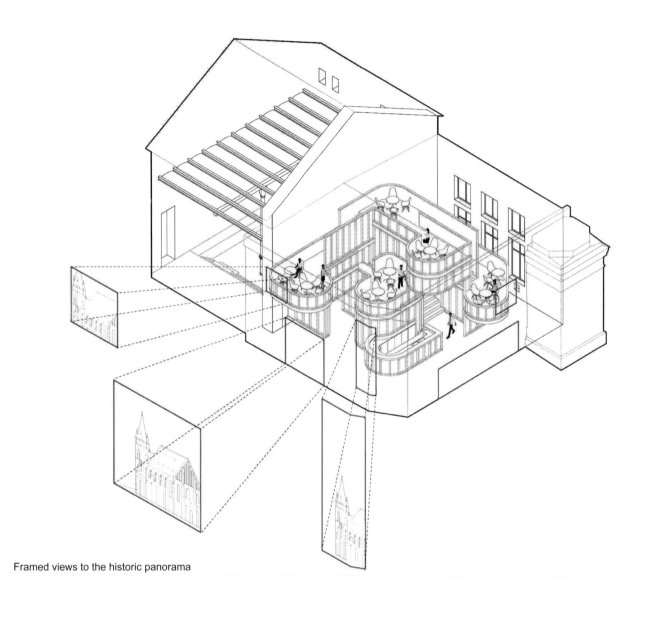

Framed views to the historic panorama

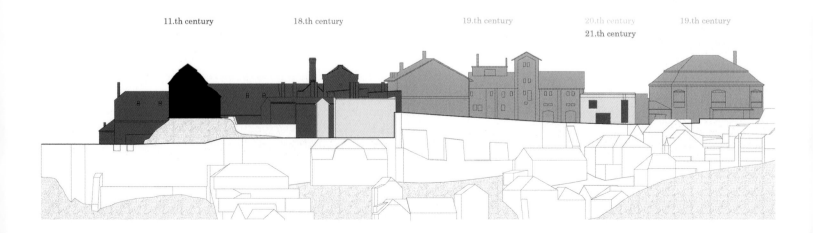

11.th century   18.th century   19.th century   20.th century   19.th century
                                                                     21.th century

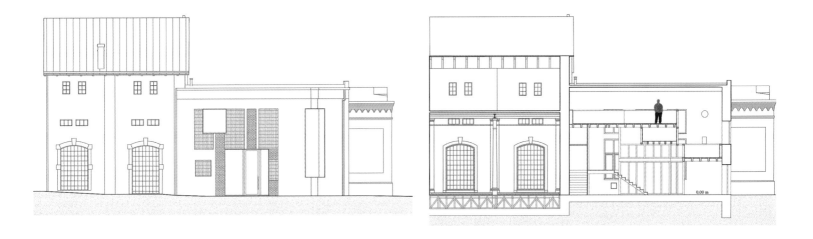

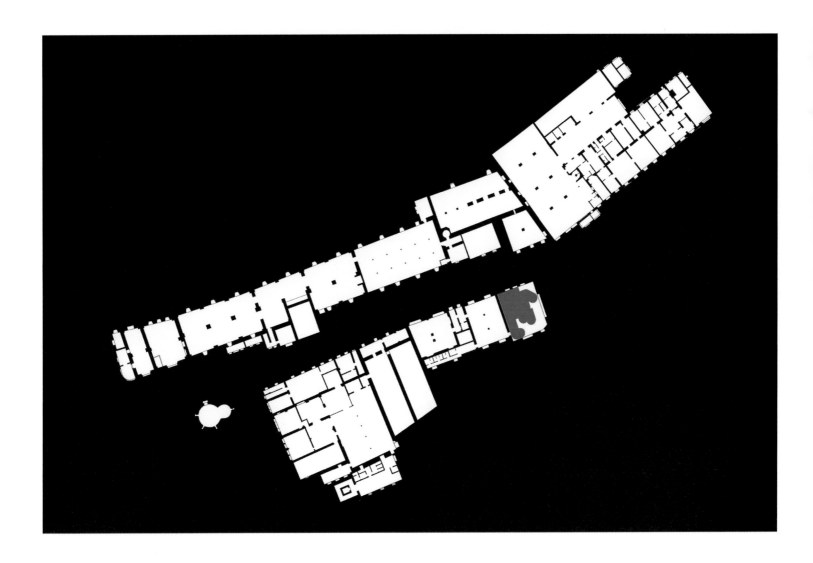

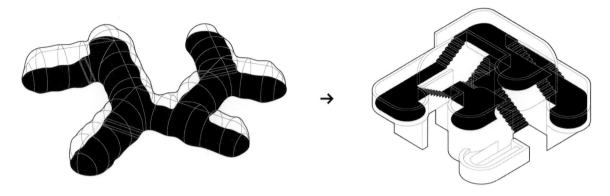

Traditional style of the wine cellar space in the region   Designed space

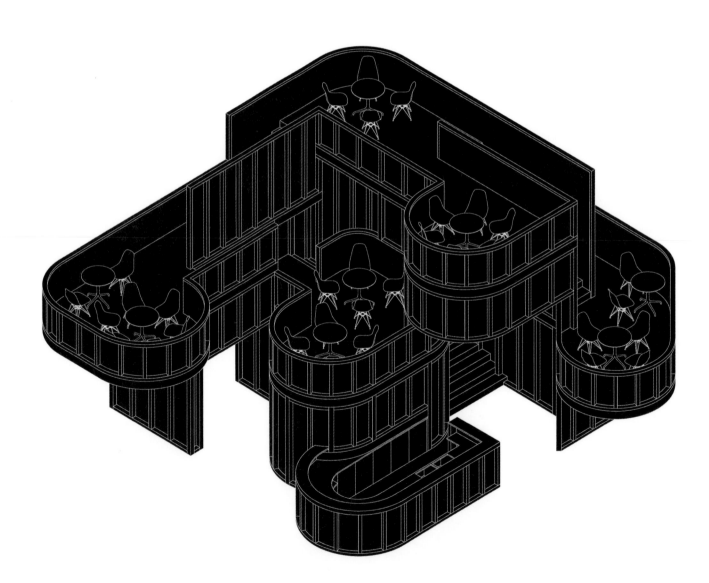

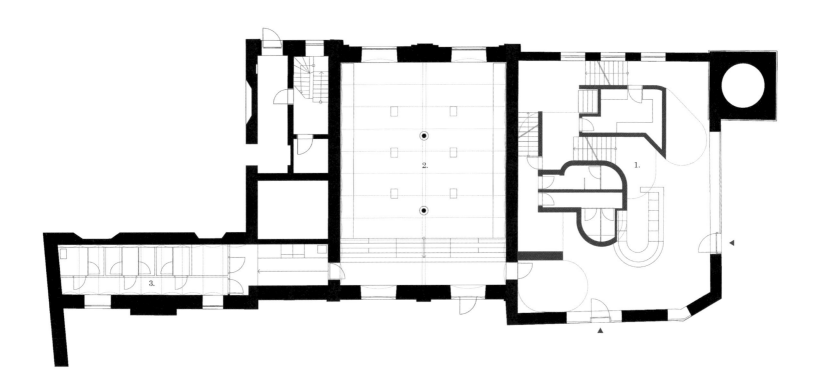

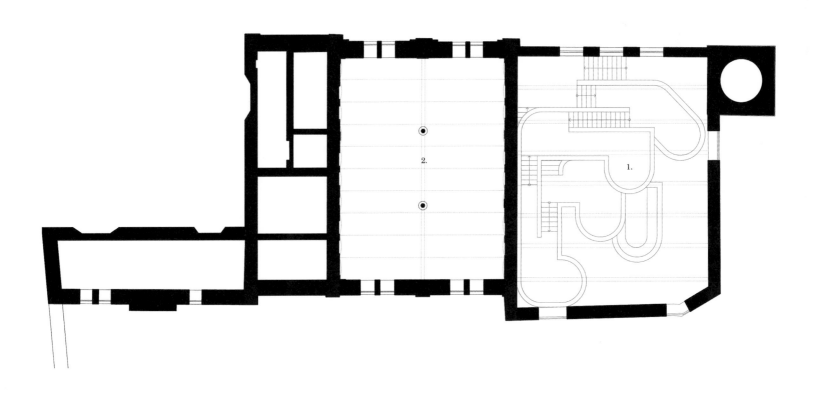

CHYBIK + KRISTOF + TEAM + MY DVA GROUP + BRNO, CZ = **GALLERY OF FURNITURE**

Year: 2015–2016
Type: office, exhibition space
Size: 550 m²
Investment: EUR 210,000
Status: completed

My new

attire

an awaite

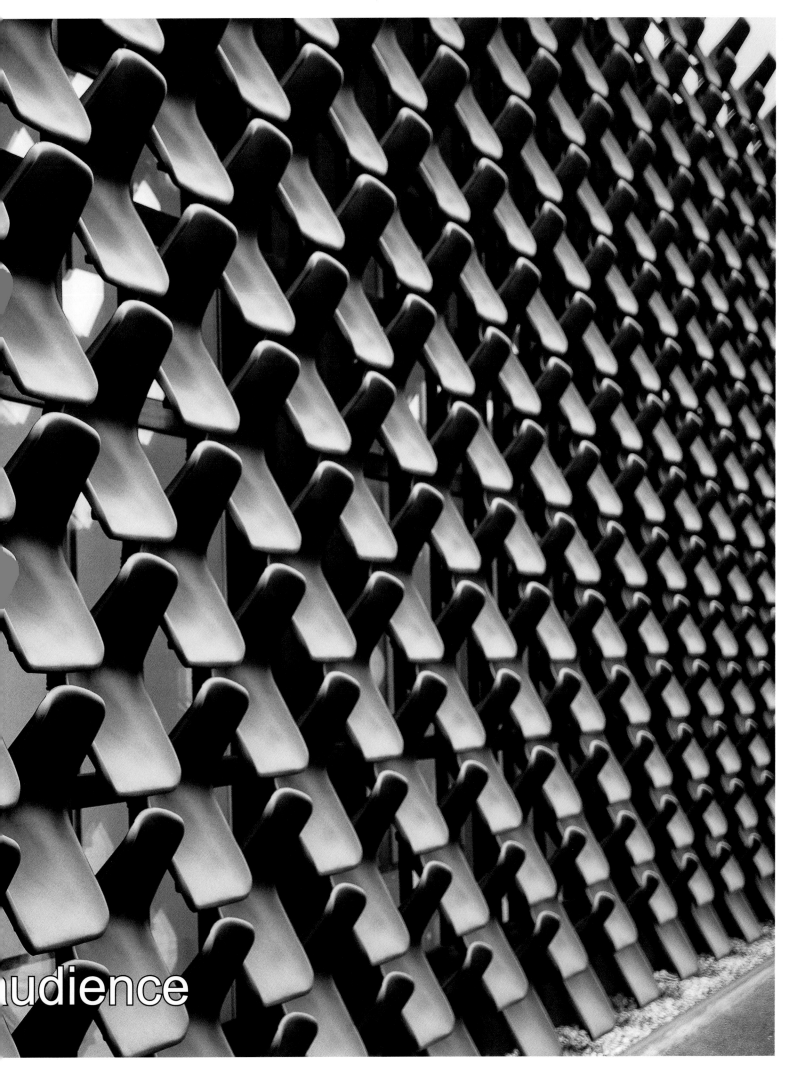

audience

the stag

s set.

The curtain

re drawn.

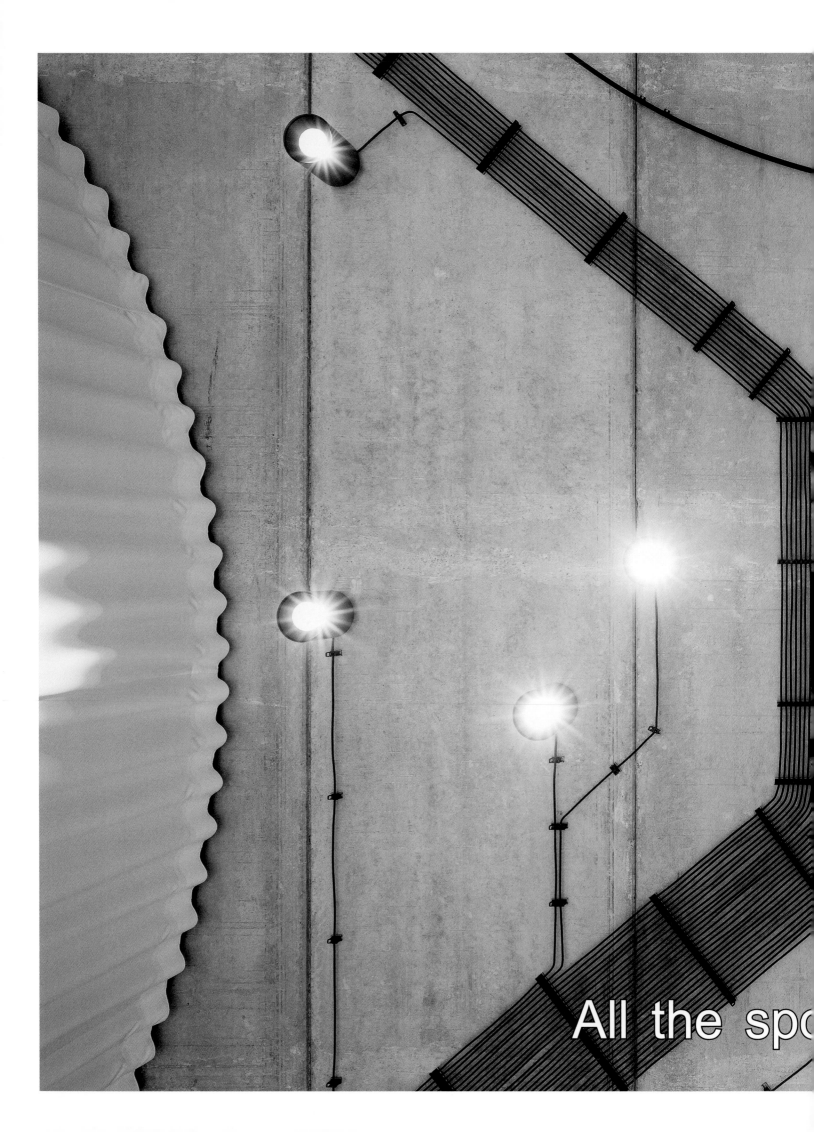

All the spo

ght on me.

Not every building out there is a gem. They don't all warrant continuous protection. As society evolves, so do our needs. Often, the structures that surround us have to be adapted and sometimes torn down. I used to operate as a run-of-the-mill car showroom with no distinct features to speak of. Unceremoniously strung along one of Brno's main radial roads, I sat empty for years and was slated for demolition before my architect's discovered me in 2015 and saw my potential.

With the firm's guidance, MY DVA Group – a leading producer and supplier of office, school and metal furniture – decided to turn me into its main salespoint. Through a simple but radical transformation, I was finally able to assert my individual identity and it had to be announced. Because the company moved in for an undetermined amount of time, my architects devised a quick and inexpensive solution that would impactfully get the word out. My otherwise unassuming exterior was rapidly transformed. The architects rendered my conventional stucco façade with a grid of 900 black plastic Vincenza chair seats – the tenant's most successful product. All of a sudden, I was taller, bolder and spoke louder. My neighbours started listening.

It seems to me that CHK doesn't follow a one-size-fits-all philosophy. Rather, the firm devises transformations on a case-by-case basis and takes all the factors of a site and its various uses into consideration before doing so. I had to leave hints informing them on which of my characteristics were most important to revitalise and which weren't; what was integral to my being and what could be morphed, reshaped or adapted.

My architects responded to all of these stipulations while still achieving cohesion. Though my exterior serves as a calling card, the real action happens inside. CHK further demonstrated its ability to implement quick and inexpensive solutions by introducing modular curtain walls and removable polycarbonate partitions that break up offices and showrooms within my minimal, open-plan volume.

The firm often solves problems like my original eyesore façade by applying audacious yet carefully calculated and considered transformations. They do so by riffing on the myriad tensions that exist between tectonic or aesthetic clarity and programmatic complexity. I'm a pure demonstration of my architect's central ethos: using the physical and intellectual tools of reuse, materiality, reconnection, historical revaluation and contextualisation to equal effect. One can look at me and say 'I know exactly what this place has to offer.'

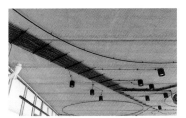
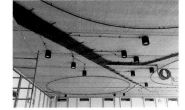
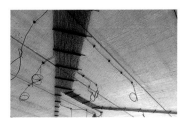

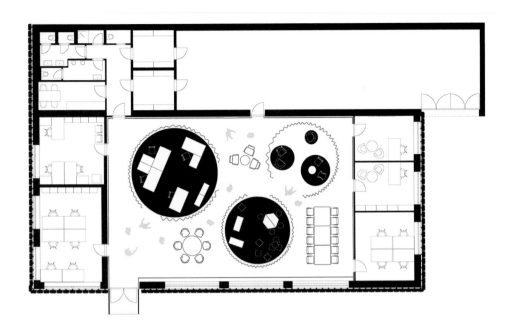

Exhibition

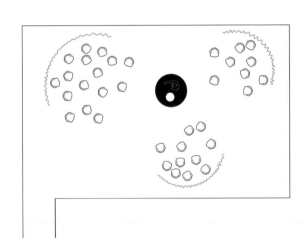

Lecture

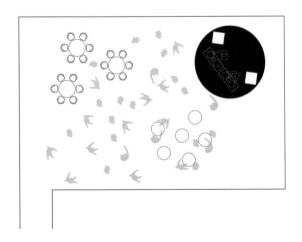

Party

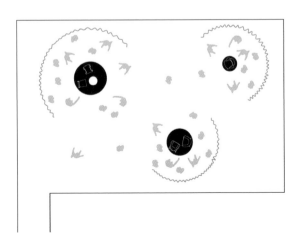

Presentation of new product

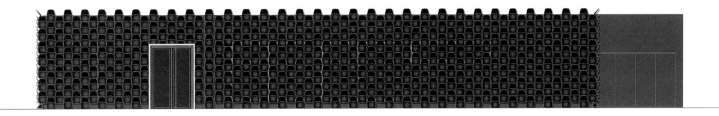

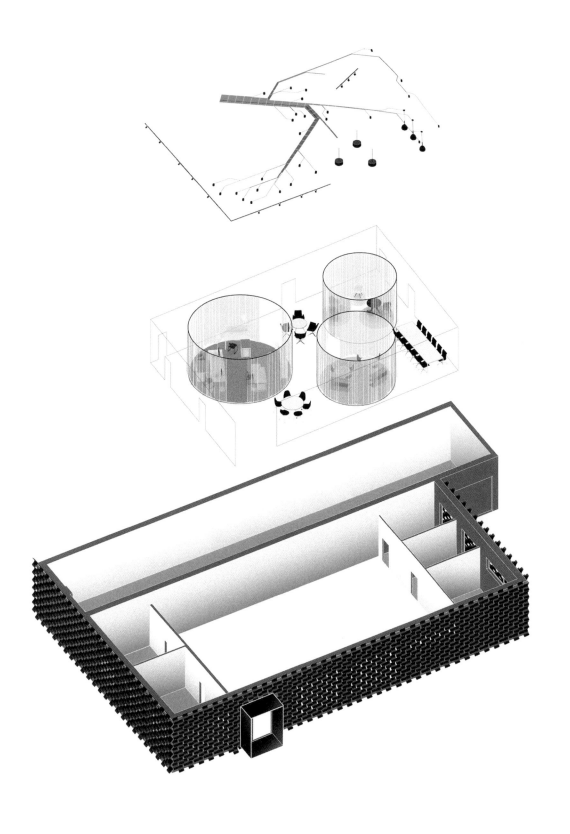

CHYBIK + KRISTOF + TEAM + CITY OF USTI NAD ORLICI + USTI NAD ORLICI, CZ = **PEARL GALLERY**

Year: 2022
Type: cultural, public space
Size: 3200 m^2
Investment: EUR 3,255,200
Status: competition (1st prize), ongoing

Letting th

past shine

I invite you to

iscover my layers

I have not

ng to hide.

With every fibr

...I'm the new

Pearl of my city.

I'm a large art space that began life as a textile factory. For the town of Usti nad Orlici, Czech Republic, I've long been a symbol of industrial prosperity; fervent activity that abruptly came to a halt in 2009. For generations of local inhabitants, I'm the place that once provided work and ensured livelihood. My sizable 3200-m² imprint cannot be ignored nor should it be. Though I no longer perform my original function as a textile factory, I remain relevant as I adopt a new purpose as a new beacon of prosperity for the town's community.

My architects set out to reconfigure my different architectural components and ensure that I integrate even further into my surroundings without taking away from what makes me so distinct. They decided to make a grand gesture and add a cut-through within my core in order to provide me with a new entrance and connect my inner courtyard with external public spaces. I'm right next to Usti nad Orlici's main square and will be able to house both cultural and commercial tenants. With two exhibition spaces, a main hall and a smaller hall, I will add to the town's already well-supplied cultural infrastructure. Though I'm set to become something entirely different, I will always represent my past.

I'm working to integrate into my physical and cultural surroundings by respecting local history and addressing new requirements. I'm looking internally to make much needed improvements and reinvent myself. My architects are meticulous in simultaneously facilitating my transformation and maintaining my symbolic value through considerations of materiality. By casting each structure in different tones and finishes, they're setting out to distinguish different uses. Layered materials from various periods were carefully analysed. While some were left intact, others were refurbished. In contrast, new interventions and additions – walls, stairs, railing and curtain walls – were created from colourful, pearl-like components to accentuate these defining characteristics. There was one non-negotiable, however. It no longer functions, but my chimney was preserved as the clearest indicator of my past function.

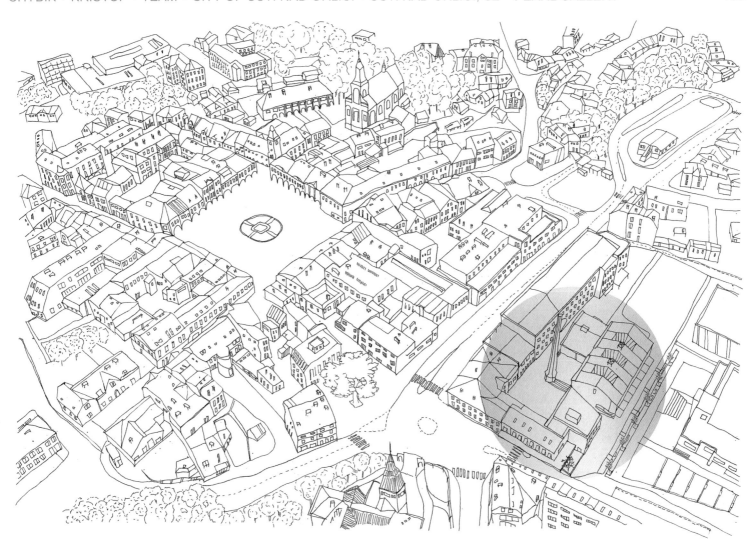

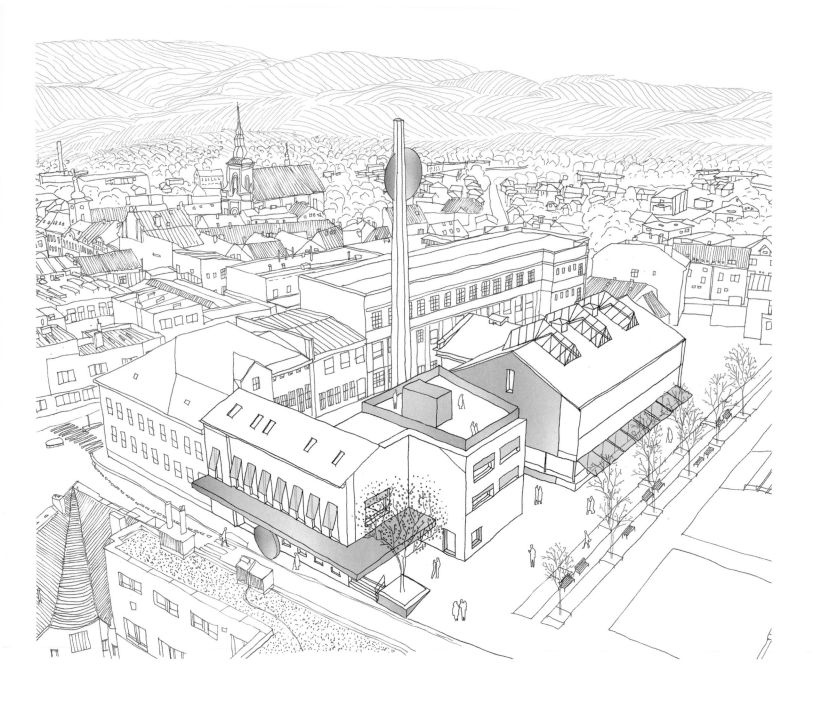

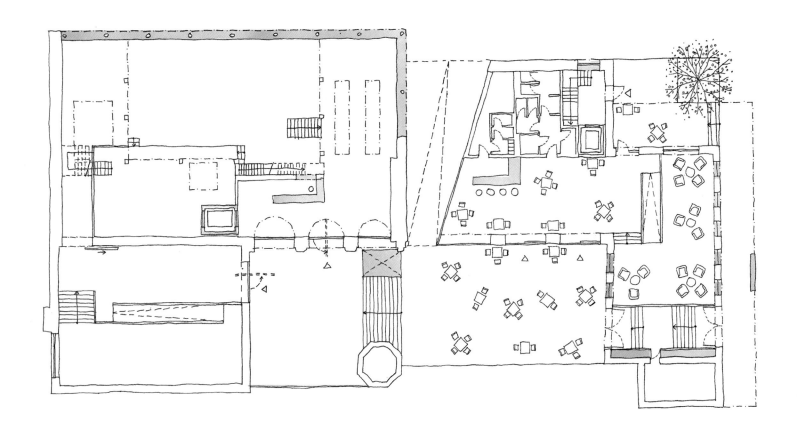

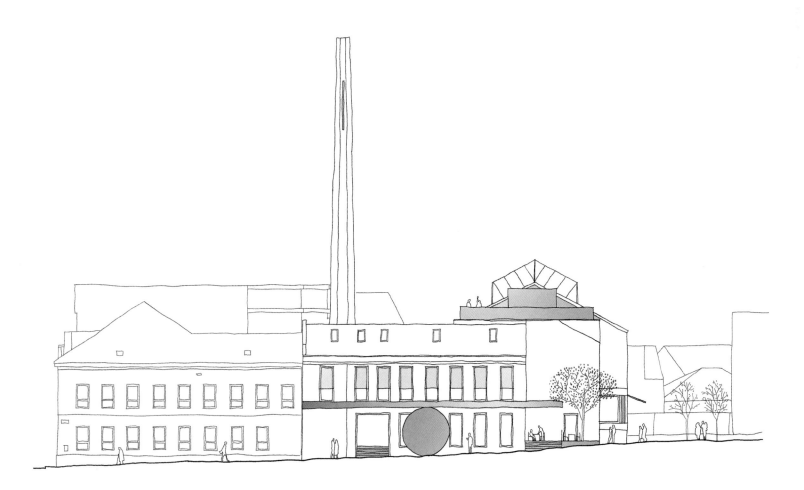

 CHYBIK + KRISTOF + TEAM + NEW YORK CITY, USA = BROADWAY ADAPTIVE REUSE

Year: 2023
Type: mixed-use, offices, residential
Size: 219,172 m²
Investment: –
Status: concept study

A legend

ack to life.

In my new playscap

o live and work.

Model of the current building condition

Addressing even the most minute design details – furnishings and finishes – my architects have implemented the principle of adaptability on all levels. The different affordable apartment typology I will include – many of which will be housed within the combined confines of old offices – are set to be kitted out with a wide choice of materials. All of these components will be upcycled from portions of my structure that are slated for demolition. Old support beams will become built-in shelves while glazing panels will become room partitions.

Will I meet everyone's needs and can I do so with as little additional environmental impact as possible? Will New Yorkers be open to what I have to offer? How could other buildings in my vicinity, those across town and even around the globe embrace a similar spirit of resourceful and responsible agility?

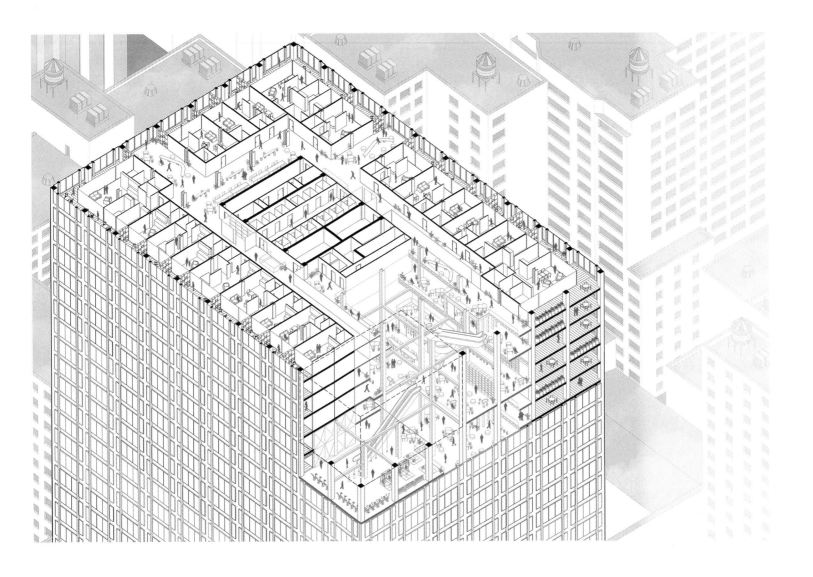

CHK has envisioned an intricate scheme that champions connectivity, integration and adaptability above all else. The architect's proposed intervention will do little to change my outward dark glass exterior and instead, make good use of the elements within my interior that can still serve a purpose. My architects have also imagined a complete reprogramming. At the forefront of consideration was the reality that numerous individuals are encountering challenges in delineating their work and personal lives. This is especially true when their already-cramped homes have to accommodate both purposes.

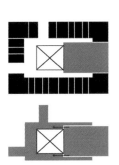

Offices

Shared spaces

Apartments

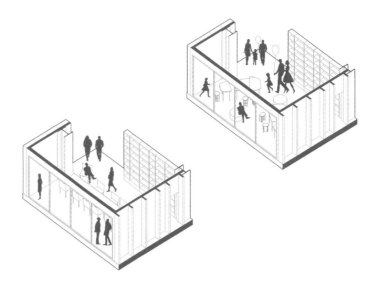

Shared spaces used for different activities

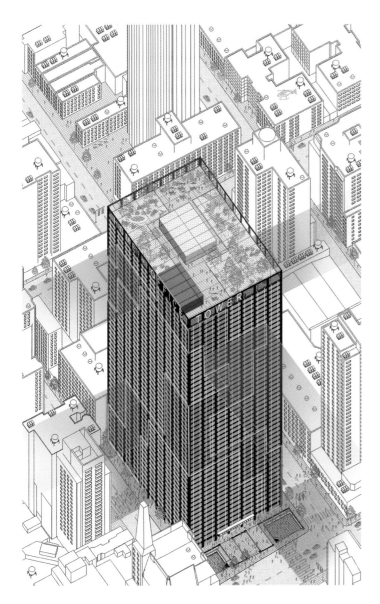

Outside: visible connectivity

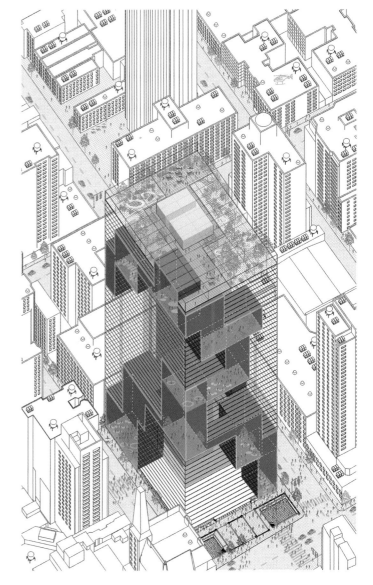

Inside: shared spaces distribution

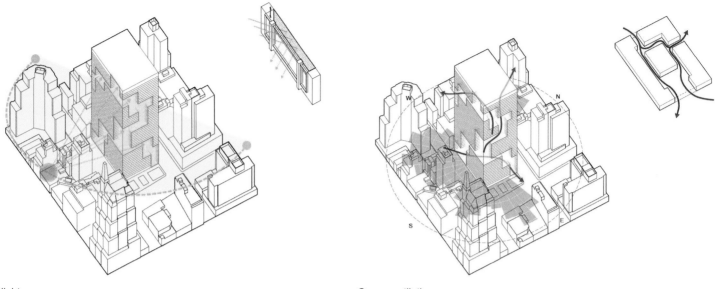

Daylight

Cross ventilation

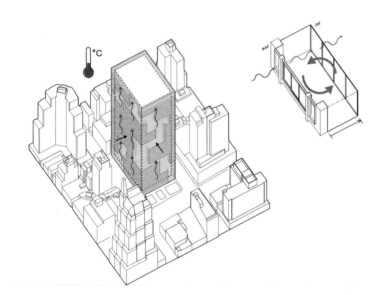

double-skin façade

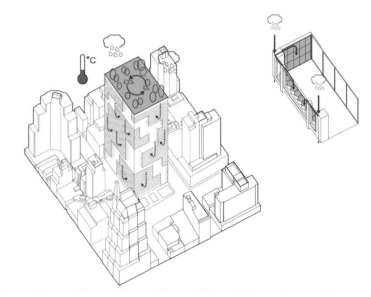

Water management

Engineered with improved daylighting, energy efficiency,
cross ventilation and innovative water management,
I will incorporate two intertwined programmes; zero-waste
ecosystems seamlessly coexisting. Inhabitants not working
on a given day don't have to engage with the spaces time-
sensitively attributed to that function. One of my floors,
alone, will be able to accommodate both programmes and
cleverly find use for areas that traditionally go dark. Meeting
rooms will moonlight as amenity spaces for various events
during evenings and weekends without holding on to any
visual reminders of the former.

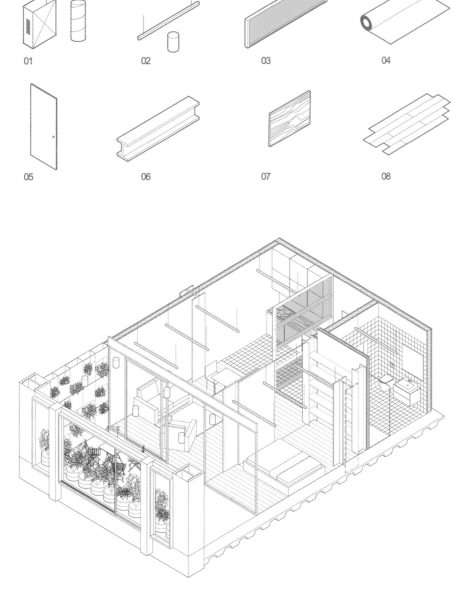

01.
HVAC pipes reused as planters and terrace partitions

02.
Reuse of lightning fixtures

03.
Façade elements that have been replaced are now employed as walls for the kitchen partition system

04.
Shredded carpets reused for acoustic insulation in the partition system

05.
Reuse of existing offices doors

06.
Residual beams used for modular shelving system

07.
Obsolete wooden elements from flooring and walls reused for kitchen counter desks

08.
Old wooden floors refurbished and reused

Typical apartment unit: zero-waste transformation

Attending to even the minutest design details – furnishings and finishes – my architects have implemented the principle of adaptability on all levels. The diverse and affordable apartment typologies I will incorporate – many of which will be housed within the combined confines of former offices – are poised to be furnished with a wide array of materials. All these elements will be upcycled from portions of my structure that are earmarked for demolition. Previous support beams will be repurposed into integrated shelves, while glazed panels will be transformed into room partitions.

Will I meet the needs of everyone, and can I do so with minimal additional environmental impact? Will the residents of New York be receptive to what I have to offer? How might other buildings in my vicinity, those across the city, and even around the globe embrace a similar ethos of resourceful and responsible agility?

CHYBIK + KRISTOF + TEAM = PUBLIC ACTORS

What does it mean for a building or urban master plan to operate as a public actor, which advocates for better accessibility and engagement rather than just answer the demands of a single stakeholder? What considerations does the design of such a vital infrastructure have to address in meeting the needs of different users; those that might engage with the space on a daily basis or those just passing through? As explored in the Vltava Philharmonic Hall proposal, developments that have such a sizable footprint within dense urban settings are obligated to accommodate different modalities. They have to situate within not only the historical fabric of a location but open up to the layers of function that activate their surroundings and maximise the possibility for interaction. Similarly, the redevelopment of the Jihlava Multipurpose Arena is set to reignite the flurry of activity the disused sports venue once experienced but also to reactivate its surroundings by reconnecting different urban fabrics. It is no longer feasible to erect structures or systems that disconnect from their context and negatively impede organic movement. Another example of this approach is also demonstrated in the revamping of Mendel Square; bold site-specific instigations should be balanced with purposeful interventions. As a simple but impactful gesture, a unifying visual element that hints to the past can be tactfully laid over a reconfigured traffic flow. In this chapter of Crafting Character, Chybik + Kristof demonstrates how buildings and spaces can become public actors by reflecting the needs, values and aspirations of the communities they serve.

 CHYBIK + KRISTOF + TEAM + MECANOO + PRAGUE INSTITUTE OF PLANNING AND DEVELOPMENT + PRAGUE, CZ = **VLTAVA PHILHARMONIC HALL**

Year: 2022
Type: culture, public space
Size: 53,220 m^2
Investment: EUR 196,000,000
Status: competition

Among th

ounds of my city

my voice

tands out

a symphon

of urban scape

rban instrument.

One might find themselves unknowingly climbing up the urban ribbon walkways that curve up to encircle the cylindrical core of my main concert hall. That's the point. No longer a venue reserved for so-called cultural elites, the many components of my urban carpet master plan are intended to perfectly integrate within Prague's street grid, providing seamless connections to pre-existing public transportation and serving as an unobstructed passageway for the different districts in my vicinity. I don't want to be an inaccessible fortress stamped in place without considerations of site specificity. I've worked hard to uncover and embody this rich complexity. It's my responsibility to serve my users in every way possible.

I was developed by Chybik + Kristof, in partnership with Dutch firm Mecanoo as part of a large international competition. They were one of the few to develop a proposal that prioritised the public; Prague's more than 1,300,000 residents moving between different neighborhoods or taking in a show at one of my venues.

If I were to have been constructed, I'd have become much more than an austere neoclassical opera house or oversized museum from the past. Too often, these institutions have been cut-off from the bustling cities they inhabit and intimidate the citizens that should be experiencing what they have to offer. My architects would have ensured that my volume could facilitate multiple functions. Not only incorporating a generous amount of space for pedestrian plazas, the cultural and social hub could have also included outdoor amphitheatres, conference centres, public foyers, exhibition spaces and so much more. They'd have used various sophisticated urban planning strategies to advocate for my public engagement. A riverfront, boulevard, courtyard, music alleyway, park, passageway, square, plaza and open building fronts would have been added to ensure my approachability. By using soft and organic shapes throughout, my architects mirrored the look and feel of the capital's historic architecture as well as the buildings that are specifically adjacent to my site.

My architects' concept not only honoured and elevated my context through the mindful use of certain forms and dynamic infrastructure but accentuated these features to great effect. Those that might have followed the gradual helix-structured ramps wrapping my concert hall might have also caught a glimpse of an orchestra performing inside.

Reflecting the Czech Republic's sizable impact on the history of glassmaking, my glazed façades would have become an intricately crafted sculpture in their own right. Audiences could have experienced perfect sound thanks to the curvilinear shape of the building, its matrix of intersecting wood panels and custom padding developed by industry leading firm Nagata Acoustics.

Existing urban art

Humanity and Work,
Jan Štursa, 1913

Faun and Vltava, Miroslav and Olga
Hudečkovi, 1984

Pedestals, Jiři Babiček, 1983

Vltava, Jan Fišar and Václav Zajic,
1984

Ceramic pipe, Aleš Werner, 1986

Ceramic wall, Václav Dolejš
and Jindra Viková, 1984

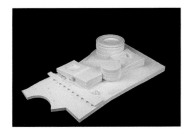 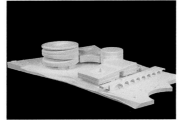 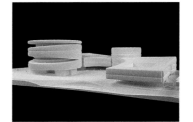 

Having the ability to serve various purposes at different times of day was another important consideration in making sure that I could be accessible to almost every individual that would have passed through. I'd have facilitated both those studying in my music library during the morning and those partying into the early hours at my waterfront bar. Nearby moorings would have welcomed concerts ships on special occasions. I'd have hosted multiple events at once without disrupting the natural movement of commuters passing through.

CHK and Mecanoo were able to develop this all-encompassing solution by carefully observing how the area is used in every way possible throughout a given day, isolating obstacles and developing multiple proposals to improve upon these various site-specific challenges in equal measure. Unfortunately, I was never constructed but the strategies used in my development could be useful in almost any other public-facing project that has to contend with multiple layers of historical and contemporary constraint.

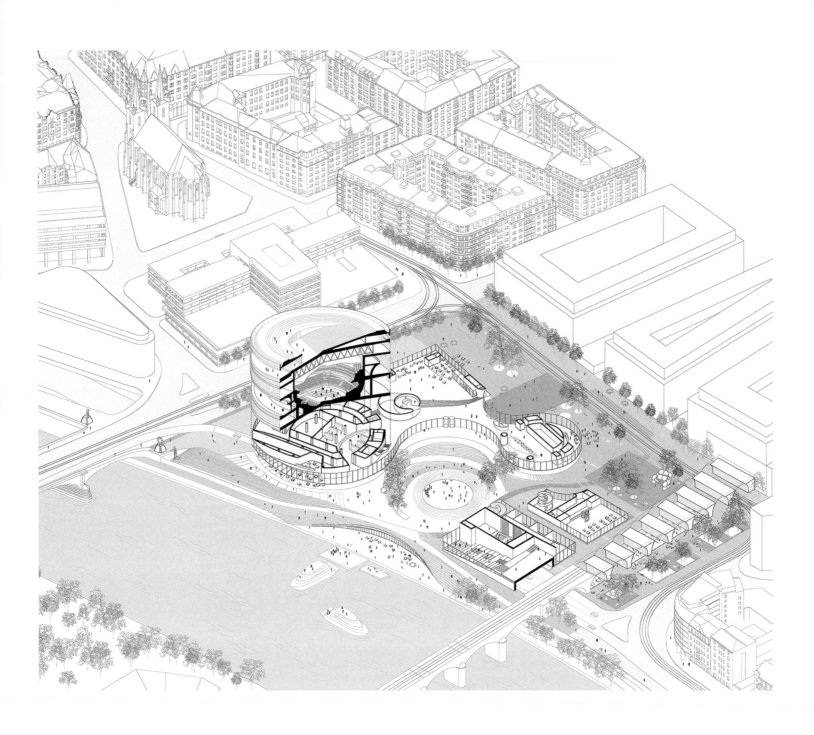

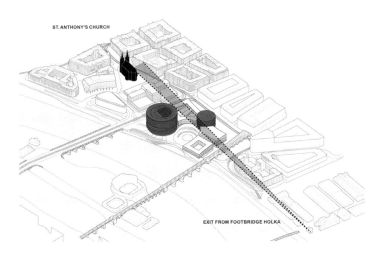

Position of halls and St. Anthony's church

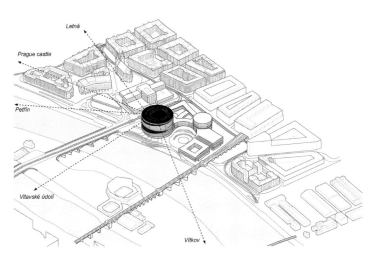

Main hall views

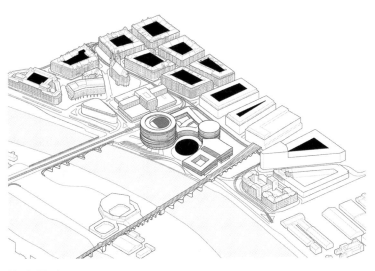

Music block

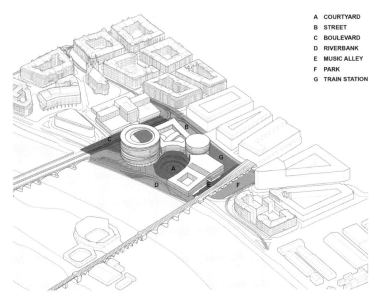

Rich typology of urban spaces

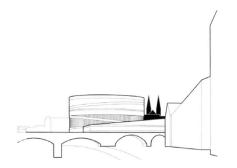

Vltava Philharmonic and St. Anthony's church

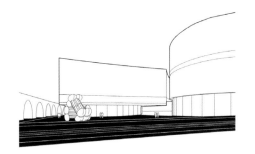

Train station square

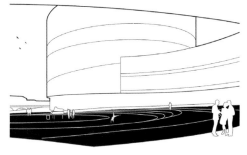

Courtyard

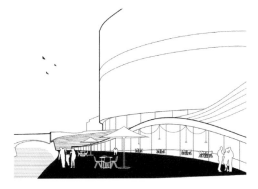

Riverbank

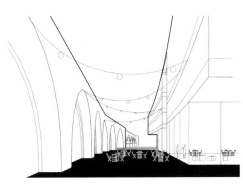

Music alley

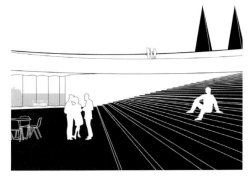

Restaurant and bistro with a view to the city

CHYBIK + KRISTOF + TEAM + MICHAL PALASCAK + ZDENEK SENDLER + BRNO, CZ = **MENDEL SQUARE**

Year: 2021–2022
Type: transformation, civic, public space
Size: 13,000 m^2
Investment: EUR 8,400,000
Status: completed

I am a square

and a circle

all around

his place.

Within the seaml

s transportation

I am a destina

on on my own.

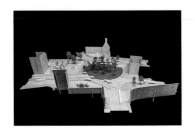

Engaging in the entire history of a site requires much more than just the rudimentary consultation of conventional textbooks or statistics. These resources almost always reflect a singular narrative or managed agenda. As a public square and transportation hub set in the heart of Brno, I'm more concerned with addressing different viewpoints and accommodating various stakeholders. After undergoing an intensive revitalisation from 2021–2022, my 13,000 m² of space now doubles as a public square and an efficient matrix of transit networks. I now welcome hundreds of daily visitors, moving swiftly between different metropolitan tram and city bus lines.

It wasn't always like this however, for too long, I was neglected and my potential overlooked. I had no direction and aimlessly blended into the rest of Brno's city grid. It's strange given that I'm the center of Staré Město, the city's oldest historical district. Around me are buildings that have had immeasurable influence on the world. Next to the 14th-century Basilica of the Assumption of Our Lady – a shining example of Moravian Gothic architecture – is the Abbey of Saint Augustin, where my namesake, Gregor Mendel, experimented with what we now know as genetics. I operated as a well-attended park for many decades but

during World War II, sustained major damages. During the communist era that preceded, characterless buildings were constructed around my perimeter. At the time, these uniform structures slowly chipped away at the common perspective of my historical significance. I barely functioned as a transit point as my users had no clear indication of where one public transportation line stopped and another started.

It wasn't until my architects – together with local partners and specialists – came into the picture, that I was brought back to my former glory. To bring my historical significance to the fore all while facilitating a better flow of commuter traffic, they decided that a bespoke and site-specific scheme would be more effective than a standard methodology.

To reclaim the public space, I was defined by a circular overlay of red stone referring to material historically excavated in the area and often used in local architecture. My restoration was completed in 2022. This textured decal moves across various levels of pavement – roads, walking paths, transportation platforms and plazas – but does not hinder the smooth movement of different bus and tram networks that pass through. Instead, this intervention precisely delimits and pinpoints where they intersect and users can transfer with clear wayfinding and little obstruction. It accomplishes this modality while also alluding back to my past. From above or even from my edges, it's clear who I am and what I do.

Adding a third layer, my core is broken up by a maximum amount of trees. This sprinkling of greenery serves travelers passing through to cool in shade but also local residents or office workers looking for a place to take a break. A strategically placed system of drains and sophisticated underground channels allows the trees' roots to stay interconnected with each other. The site-specific solution reflects my future-forward, ecological ambitions. As an added bonus, I incorporate modular benches that accommodate various needs at different times of day.

As a monument commemorating Mendel's achievement in genetic research, I inform everyday visitors about the fundamental impact my immediate surroundings have had on the development of science. Though I now have a strong, defined personality that is rooted in both my past and present, you can find me negotiating between different layers of activity at any time of day. I'm an individual and stand out in so many ways but most importantly I integrate into Brno's urban landscape and fulfill my role to the public in many ways more than before.

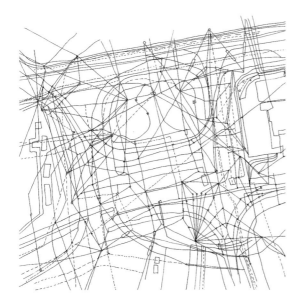

Existing infrastructure under and above ground

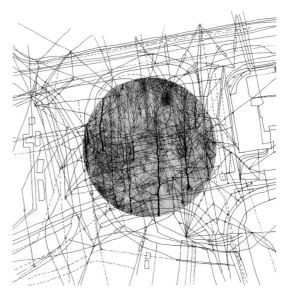

New definition of urban space

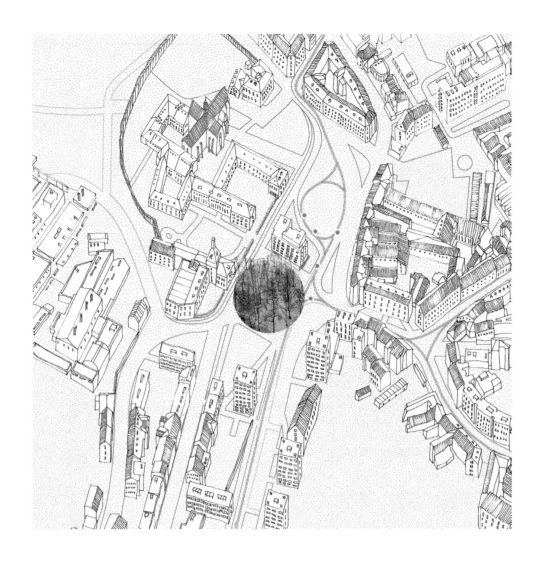

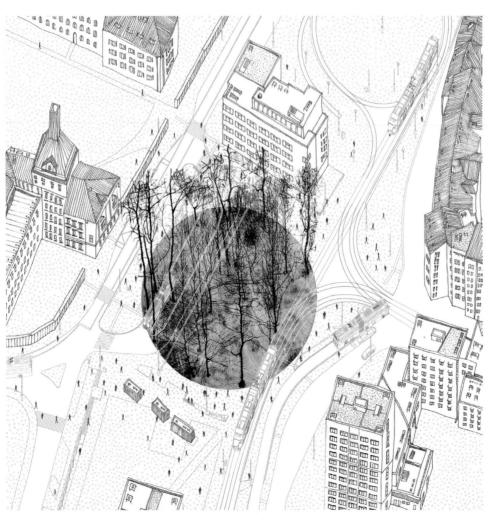

A system of drains and underground channels allows trees' roots to be connected

CHYBIK + KRISTOF + TEAM + CITY OF JIHLAVA + JIHLAVA, CZ = JIHLAVA MULTIPURPOSE ARENA

Year: 2019
Type: mixed-use, sport, civic
Size: 25,000 m²
Investment: EUR 30,000,000
Status: competition (1st prize), ongoing

I get my energy

rom the city

rooted i

his place

with a goa

hat unites us

when we a

gather here

I want to show

I'm an ur

n beacon.

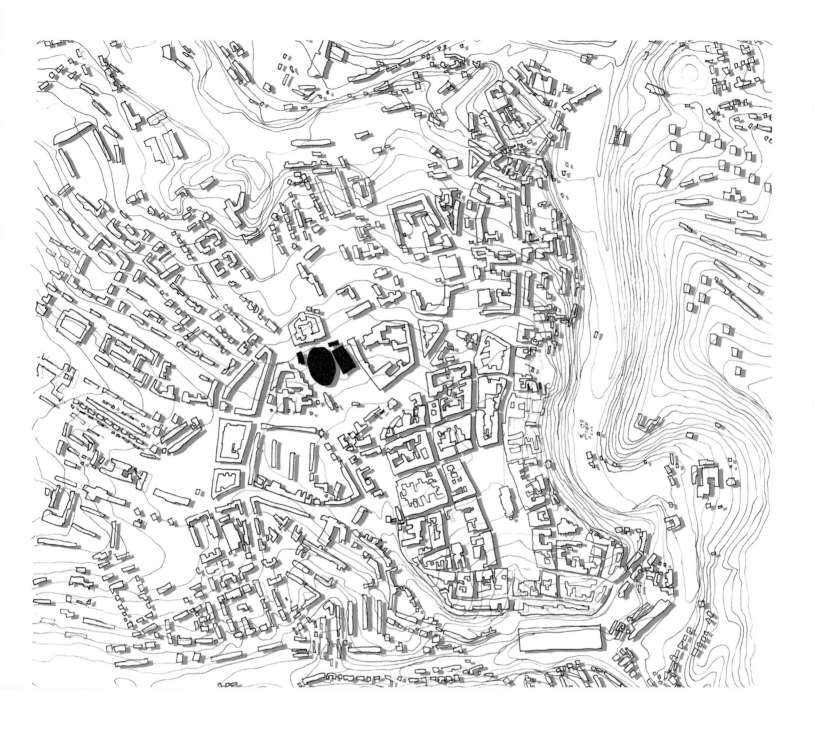

I was first constructed in the 1950s as an enclosed hockey rink but by the 2020s, my walls and roof were crumbling and I no longer reflected the needs of the surrounding community. If you look at most major sporting venues throughout the world, they sit on the outskirts of town. I am situated in the centre of Jihlava, Czech Republic, and it is imperative that I become more reflective of its citizens and their distinct values. Moreover, it holds great significance for my architects to ensure that I am reprogrammed in a way that promotes and fosters the economic growth of my city. I'm set to become a place that will not only host various sports events but also accommodate the city's social and generational diversity. I need to be both an internal cultural meeting point and a calling card communicating my message to the rest of the country and the world.

Winning a competition for my redevelopment, my architects envisioned a new scheme that would facilitate a broad spectrum of activities for different audiences. I will no longer be just one structure, but rather a complex of four buildings that will enable me to integrate better within my surroundings. Joining my cylindrical stadium are connected rectilinear volumes that will facilitate different functions. When completed, I will represent the dynamic interplay of spatial efficiency and strong aesthetic qualities that will set me apart.

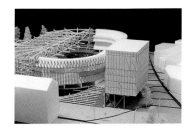

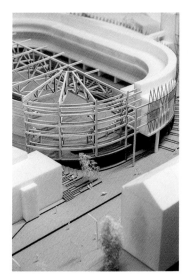

I'll be able to simultaneously honour my history and accommodate contemporary needs. I'll be widely accessible to those that will use me for various purposes on a daily basis and recognisable to those visiting from out of town. It isn't mutually exclusive. It's about maintaining the distinct characteristics that'll inspire them to come in the first place. One ends up benefiting the other. This is a quality my constituents will be proud of and something that will become more emboldened to re-engage with especially as I yet again host the widely supported local hockey club. For me, the very idea of being a public actor is defined by distilling needs and addressing them with emphatic resolve.

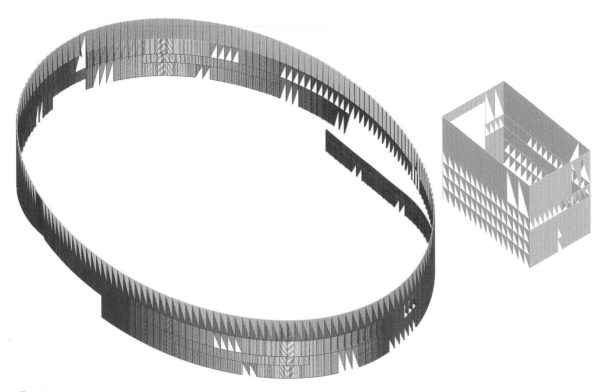

Façade system

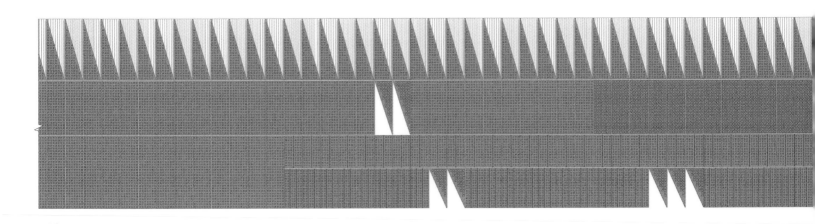

Unwrapped façade: street gate

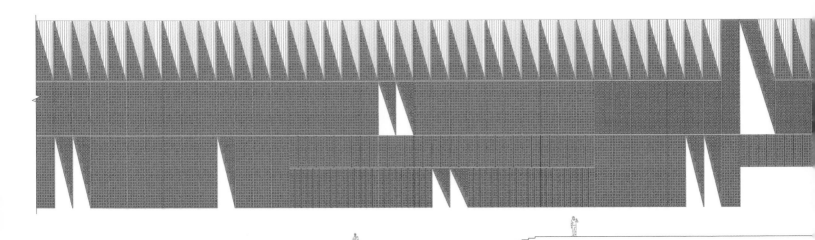

Unwrapped façade: park gate

Children's image of Jihlava Multipurpose Arena

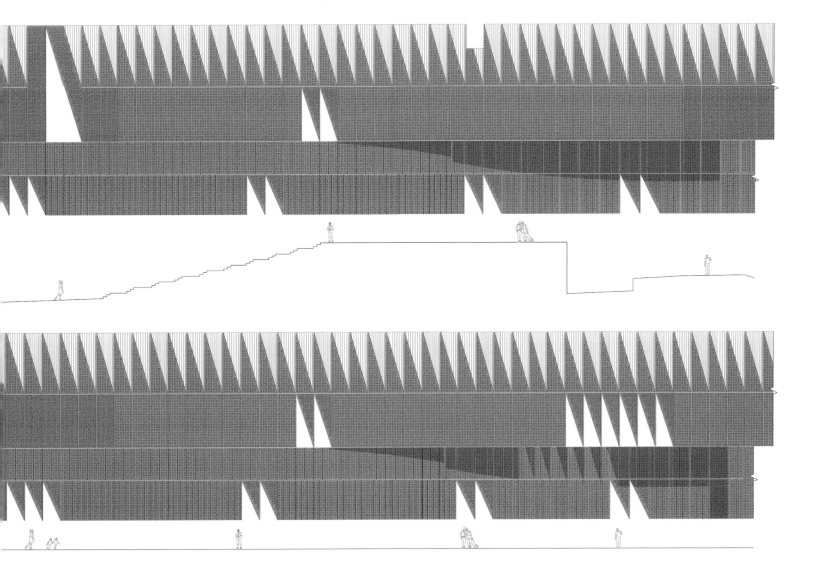

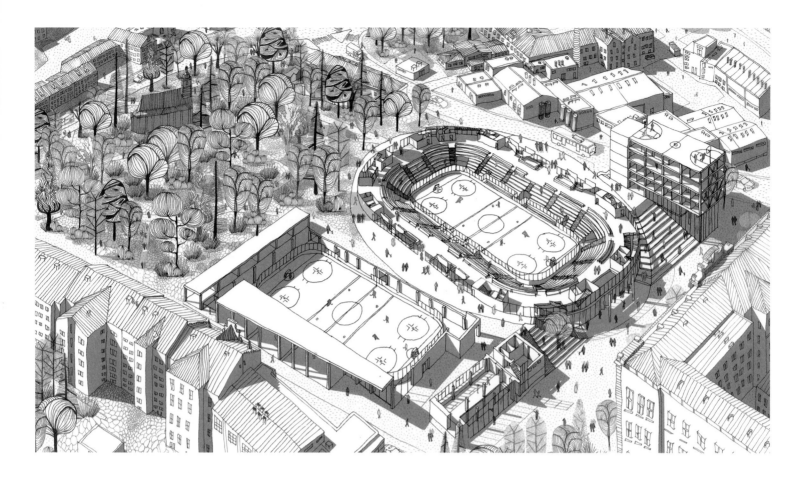

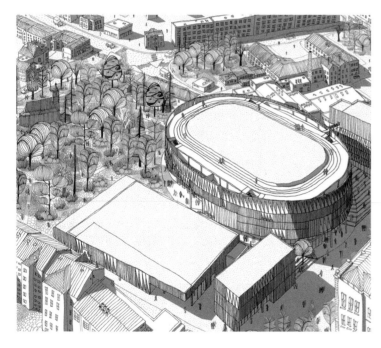

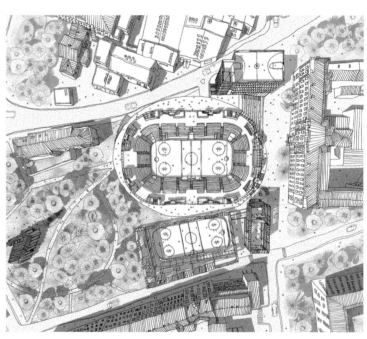

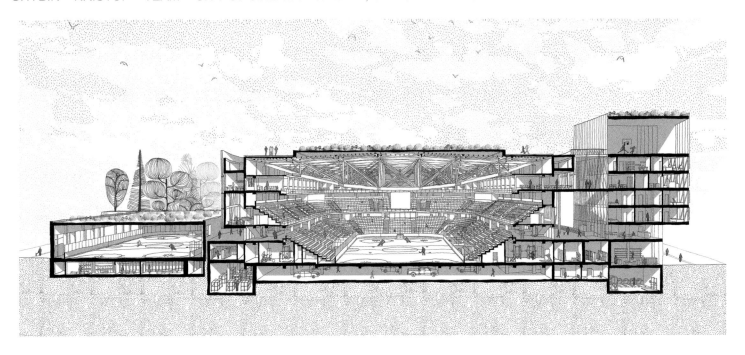

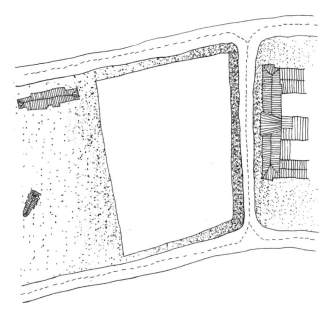

Existing stadium: flow interrupted

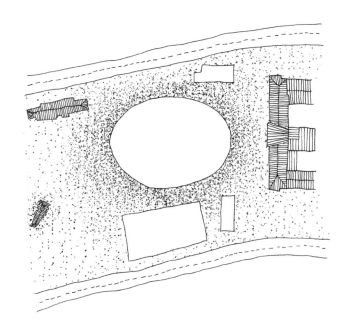

New stadium: fluid transition

CHYBIK + KRISTOF + TEAM = PREFABRICATED MODULARITY

As human beings, we're constantly engaging in some form of modification or other. In a bid to ensure our own survival and relevance, we're always finding new ways to change our behaviour and confront the latest challenges. Adaptation is not merely predicated on a singular entity's gradual evolution but also the mediation of different requirements. This principle allows us to cohabitate with other people and even non-human life forces. In our present day, architects are increasingly and consciously experimenting with modularity and prefabrication in order to push the boundaries of traditional construction methodologies and explore new possibilities.

Architecture is at its best when facilitating flexibility. Prefabrication and modularity allows for innovative solutions to be quickly applied in almost any context, especially those set to become increasingly complex in the future. Such programmatic and structural frameworks are open enough to accommodate quick modifications, adjustments and even fully fledged adaptive reuse schemes. Prefabrication and modularity can also account for significant environmental benefits: reduced waste generation, quicker construction timelines, minimal on-site disturbances and positive impact on both embodied and operational carbon emissions. Architects have the advantage of better controlling the use of materials as standardised components are carefully researched, kitted out and utilised. In this chapter of Crafting Character, Chybik + Kristof harnesses the power of these two approaches, allowing a structure like Modular Research Center to naturally evolve over time without additional effort or financial burden.

CHYBIK + KRISTOF + TEAM + KOMA MODULAR + VIZOVICE, CZ = **MODULAR RESEARCH CENTER**

Year: 2017–2021
Type: office
Size: 170 m²
Investment: EUR 1,500,000
Status: completed

I could be here for

while or just a short time.

Forming space

or your ideas

thou

tfully.

collab

atively.

I'm made up of rectilinear modules that have been non-uniformly positioned so as to demarcate an internal courtyard. The six units were pre-fabricated and easily installed on my site using a standard crane. The 170 m² of space they incorporate serve as an office for think tank KOMA Modular, the same company that develops these components based on a design concept devised by my architects.

Together, both firms are aiming to shake up the modular architecture market by introducing concepts that are transparent, diverse and open. I'm the result. Though I've been assembled in this location as a functioning prototype, my kitted-out elements could be introduced almost anywhere and in response to almost any brief; be it a small home or a large interconnected campus. I'm adaptable.

Installed onto easily prepared foundations, my floors, walls and roof elements are smoothly aligned into position, forming a welcoming environment within a matter of hours. When put together, my components can be used for a wide range of purposes. With my modules operating as both my façade and structural column, I can support a vast array of canopy designs and cut-out exposures. In my current position, I balance the iridescence of my metallic exterior with large glass apertures and geometric skylights. My appearance is a direct result of my construction – no additional layer or ornament was added. Inside and outside, I'm truly expressing my modularity.

What sets me apart is the distilled formal vocabulary I embody and that allows me to be both flexible and aesthetically neutral. I play host to an open-plan layout that moves in different captivating directions but that also encapsulates a range of private and public areas equipped with horizontal and vertical workspaces. I've been outfitted with minimal, modular furniture that can be easily reconfigured, removed and replaced. This strategy not only aligns with my owner's ethos but helps them quickly adjust to changes in staff numbers and address employees' needs.

I'm not only an enclosed interior but also a delimited outdoor environment that my users have direct access to throughout the day. In many ways, they get two spaces for the price of one. I'm not just another large volume taking over an empty plot. My simple design is unobtrusive. My construction is feasible, inexpensive and even limited in terms of embodied and operational environmental impact. With this in mind, what else could I become? How could my modular elements or perhaps even the methodology I embody be implemented elsewhere? What other forms could I take?

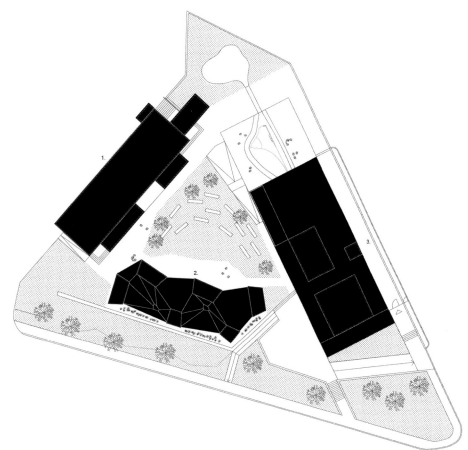

Site plan:
1. Modular cafeteria
2. Modular Research Center
3. Czech Expo Pavilion

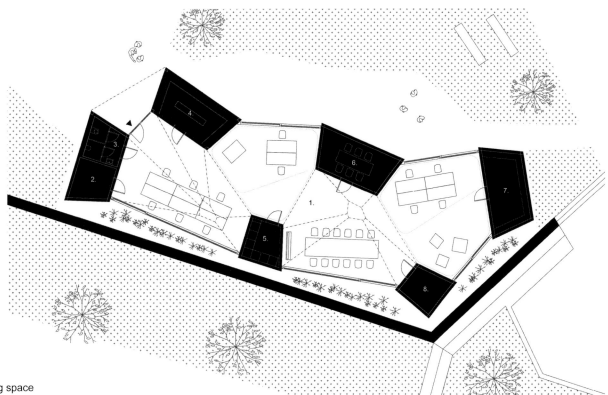

1. Coworking space
2. Utility room
3. Toilets
4. Cloakroom
5. Kitchen
6. Multimedia room
7. Samples room
8. Storage

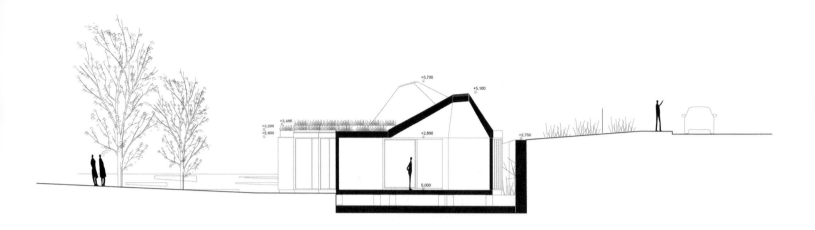

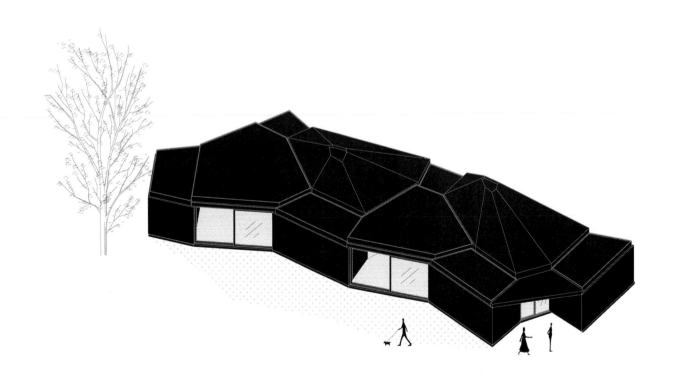

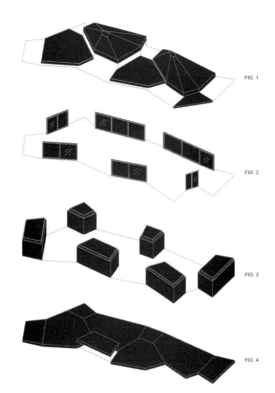

FIG. 1. Roof modules
FIG. 2. Windows
FIG. 3. Spatial modules
FIG. 4. Floor modules

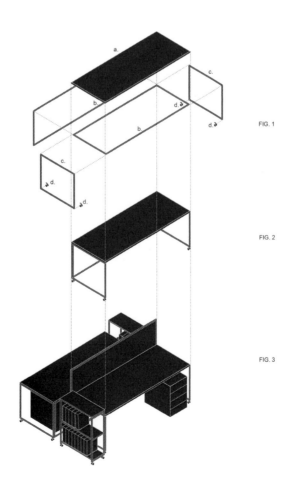

FIG. 1. Components
FIG. 2. Table
FIG. 3. Furniture set

CHYBIK + KRISTOF + TEAM = AFFORDABILITY

Most cities today are facing affordable housing crises. Population growth and the unchecked increase in real estate speculation has made living in urban downtowns financially unattainable for many. In the past, lower income developments were built on the edges of cities with no real connection to the centres and with cheap yet quickly deteriorating materials. Chybik + Kristof believes that to find viable solutions for affordable housing, architects should look past traditional ways of being cost effective and implement new strategies that better reflect society's changing needs. As evident in the Municipal Affordable Housing project, conceived for the city of Brno, flexible layouts can be the key. Instead of residing in standardised units, tenants have the ability to adapt their homes according to their requirements. All of this can be achieved without having to forsake the quality of building components. Creating common spaces within a building can also extend the functionality of even the smallest apartments.

City governments should harness the potential of disused infrastructure and empty plots to spearhead the provision of new affordable housing. Rather than allow for new luxury developments to overrun their downtowns, municipalities can amplify the qualities of densification – implementing methodologies like urban infill – to enliven their core districts. Architects can also play a critical role in imagining tailor-made solutions for each site. By accommodating all types of city dweller in the shared experience of urban life, these towns and cities can help push back the tide of community disengagement. In this chapter of Crafting Character, Chybik + Kristof makes its case for new approaches to ensuring affordable housing.

 CHYBIK + KRISTOF + TEAM + MUNICIPALITY OF BRNO + BRNO, CZ = **MUNICIPAL AFFORDABLE HOUSING**

Year: 2017–2025
Type: affordable housing
Size: 10,362 m^2
Investment: EUR 20,900,000
Status: competition (1st prize), ongoing

I found a pl

e for myself

within variou

destinations

I'm here for mea

ngful connections

I'm a

extrovert.

I'm a

ntrovert.

Like in a lot of places around the world, there's a severe lack of affordable housing in Brno. When completed, I plan to provide city dwellers with 90 new apartment units within 6 mixed-use buildings. I'm a far cry from the standard housing developments you might find throughout the United States, UK and the Czech Republic. As an urban infill, instead of being pushed out to the edge of town, I will be seamlessly interwoven within the city's core urban fabric and help densify a part of downtown Brno. My green lung courtyard will facilitate an easy flow between public and private space. I will not just be programmed for my residents but for other citizens and passersby as well. My look and feel will be similar to that of other well-rooted housing estates dotted around Brno. Every aspect of my future-forward scheme was developed by Chybik + Kristof in close partnership with local government.

Through a new inclusive economic concept, young tenants will be able to put their rent toward eventual homeownership. Living in the highly sought-after centre of the city will no longer be a luxury. Within the complex of my six housing blocks, I will feature a series of multipurpose community amenity spaces allowing my renters to activate areas other than their own domestic environments. Roof terraces and common rooms off the central staircases will act as extensions of their apartments. Beside standard flat dimensions, these units will feature movable walls that enable the ability to shift between closed private quarters (such as bedrooms) to larger open spaces that can accommodate evolving needs on a given day or over time. I'm all about internal flexibility and meeting the centre specificity of each of my many inhabitants. One does not need to infringe on another to be comfortable.

I will empower my residents to make their own decisions. They will have the opportunity to alter the layout of their units as they see fit. This approach will help them put down roots and establish a sense of home. I'm also making sure that they feel as though they can play a role in the wider Brno community. In many ways, flexibility of the apartments and accessibility to common spaces complement the concept of affordability. This dynamic and resourceful approach challenges outdated development patterns and works toward solving the global housing crisis.

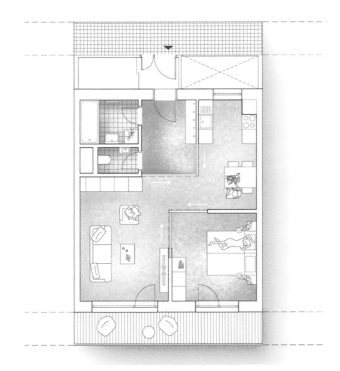

Privacy of the room

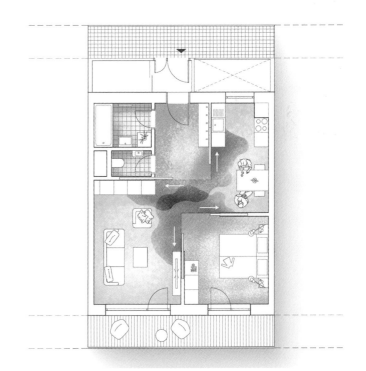

Thriving family life

CHYBIK + KRISTOF + TEAM = INTEGRATION

In architecture and urban design, integration is defined as a dialogue between two or more parties with equal interest in the success of a project. For architects – like community actors – it's about creating space for unconstrained exchange. As with other facets of placemaking – creating new buildings or environments that more closely reflect the surroundings they're set to inhabit – the idea of assimilation relies on a project's ability to incorporate ingrained traits specific to those sites while also paying close attention to intersecting layers of programmatic demands. Mendel's Greenhouse is an ode to what once stood in its place but has now taken on a more agile role. While the new structure alludes to the form of the historic greenhouse and is built upon its original foundations, it also emerges as a forum for discourse between religion and science; for the monks and the public; for scientists and new generations of learners.

Integration often lends itself to complementary methodologies such as adaptation and transformation. It can imbue historic sites with a sense of renewed function and durability. In this chapter of Crafting Character, Chybik + Kristof's interventions not only reflect the importance of function and aesthetics but also the power of harmonious integration; carefully situating a project in its environmental and cultural surroundings.

CHYBIK + KRISTOF + TEAM + ST. AUGUSTIN ABBEY IN BRNO + BRNO, CZ = MENDEL'S GREENHOUSE

Year: 2019
Type: cultural, public space
Size: 160 m²
Investment: EUR 1,100,000
Status: completed

Within thos

hallowed walls

I reflect m

predecessor

Our story i

n my genes

I'm revealing

to you.

Unde

my veil...

...we can flo

sh together.

Built on the foundations of a 19th-century glasshouse in which famed friar and scientist Gregor Mendel conducted experiments that lead to what we now call genetics, I stand as a testament to the forward-thinking and innovative spirit he embodied. In my current position, I've provided my current stewards with the chance to be more inclusive and accessible, welcoming in both the wider community of Brno, individuals from the Moravian region, the global Augustinian order and visitors from around the world. The original greenhouse that occupied the same 160 m^2 of my footprint was erected in the gardens behind the 14th-century St. Augustin Abbey in the early 1800s. It was devastated in a storm in 1870. As a reconstitute structure, I preserve the essence of the original. Because of Mendel's contribution to science and as a way to celebrate what would have been his 200th birthday, I was erected as a monument, open attraction, to bring his legacy closer to the local population, commemorate him as a local hero and identify him as an important part of the regional identity.

Though my open frame construction demonstrates the latest innovative building technologies, my DNA is quite literally a physical palimpsest of my predecessor. I was re-established by my architects using a minimal-profile steel beam and X-brace cable matrix that comprises a large-pitched roof and low-lying walls to directly reflect the trapezoidal shape of the original greenhouse. Taking this reference a step further, the very proportioning of my steel and predominantly glass enclosure manifests Mendel's three laws of inheritance. My open layout and modular shade system allows me to be versatile; to operate as a conference centre, an exhibition hall and gathering point for scientists. Nobel Prize nominees, monks, mothers with children, senior citizens – anyone, during different seasons and times of day. As an added aesthetic and conceptual value, my greenhouse is also currently being used for aeroponic farming. Permanently hung from the ceiling in silver pots, pea plants allude back to Mendel's research.

I look outward to usher in the public and help promote the various attractions that make use of my structure. I'm not concerned with asserting my own ego. Rather, CHK programmed me to frame my surroundings and entice visitors to stay longer, and go deeper into the abbey's thriving gardens. Through my very being and the principles I embody, I hope they're able to gain a tangible understanding of the critical discoveries that were made here. I've emerged from the memory of a place that once existed.

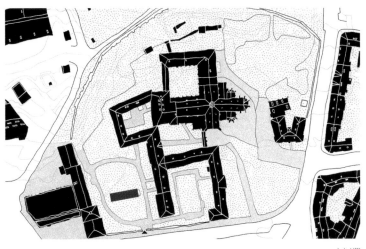

New greenhouse placed on the historical foundations

The new volume inspired by the historical greenhouse's

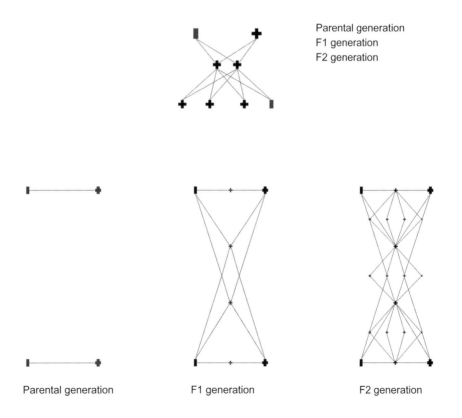

Parental generation
F1 generation
F2 generation

Parental generation   F1 generation   F2 generation

Mendel's laws of inheritance applied to the structural system

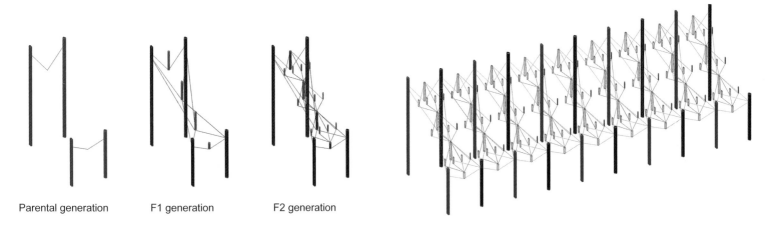

Parental generation   F1 generation   F2 generation

Mendel's laws of expressed in the structure

CHYBIK + KRISTOF + TEAM = MATERIALITY

Stand-alone structures and urban master plans can integrate into their surroundings through the thoughtful use of building materials. Adding to the aesthetic and formal quality of a project, visible elements derived from the history ecology, and past purposes of a site can help a new structure get acclimated. Having an understanding of a wide range of material properties can serve as an important source of inspiration. As evident in ongoing revitalisation schemes like the Sugar Factory, upcycling the remains of a building is not only a sustainable solution that reduces embodied environmental impact but also helps tether a project to the structures that once stood in its place. It's a transitional approach that harnesses various contextual characteristics to maintain authenticity and community engagement. The Forestry in the Forest project achieves this by employing natural materials that grow nearby, ensuring a more fluid indoor and outdoor connection. Too often, buildings are constructed without addressing the true specificities of a site, ignoring the traits that are inherent to their context and that might even be advantageous to their future success. In this chapter of Crafting Character, materiality emerges within Chybik + Kristof's work as the celebration of craftsmanship and expert selection.

CHYBIK + KRISTOF + TEAM + SKANSKA + PRAGUE, CZ = **SUGAR FACTORY**

Year: 2016–2030
Type: residential, public space, retail, landscape
Size: 58,000 m²
Investment: EUR 1,900,000,000
Status: invited competition (1st prize), under construction

Traces o

ny past

within a new

eneration.

As a central fi

re of this place

I'm whispering

ny tales to you.

Located on the outskirts of Prague, I used to produce the sweet substance that is so essential to all of our favourite treats. Unfortunately, after years of successful production and prosperity for my owners and workers, I was shut down. With no clear idea of what I might become, I turned into a brownfield site. My neighbours, however, were not content with seeing me fall into such disarray. They banded together and decided that my large footprint should be converted into a mixed-use campus. My architects listened and now, I'm set to incorporate various cultural, commercial and residential facilities while seamlessly integrating into my surroundings with new public spaces. Riverfront park and new central plaza will be the first of its kind in the district created for both existing and new inhabitants. These concerned citizens continue to play an important role in shaping my transformation. A temporary public space for the community has been erected while the rest of my master plan is realised.

Envisioning a new design, my architects teamed up with a real estate developer to develop a scheme that will ensure my relevance for contemporary and future living. Notably, the collaborative effort between them has resulted in the production of a bespoke façade material called Rebetong. The new component is made from a composite of recycled brick and concrete sourced from the demolition of the factory buildings that used to occupy my location. They decided to take on this holistic approach as a way to reduce waste, have a smaller carbon footprint and incur fewer construction costs, but also to infuse me with the physical essence of my predecessor. I will be intrinsically linked to the former complex and its history. In many ways, I'm the factory's reincarnation.

On completion, inhabitants in my close to 800 apartments will have retail spaces, a brewery, a restaurant, a kindergarten, a boat club and an enclosed multifunctional community space which can serve as an open air theatre, marketplace, gathering point and so much more. This will all be incorporated thanks to CHK's careful park and plaza planning: an intricate layout of gardens, fields, walkways, benches and pagodas that seamlessly transition between private and public activities. The master plan translates from the blue-green infrastructure model that symbiotically incorporates waterway stewardship with ground-based landscaping.

A lot of CHK's concept works with – and accentuates – the biodiversity that's already in place. On top of that, I will be imbued with an embedded infrastructure that optimises my water management. Accompanying my use of renewable energy, this system will work to bolster my carbon neutrality. I'll incorporate a rich layering of materials that are specific to my surroundings, an approach that was essential to my revitalisation as it could be in many other scenarios.

What should new mixed-use developments offer their tenants? How should they embody the past of the locations they emerge from? How can architects and construction companies begin to re-imagine how they implement material? Could sourcing and reprocessing raw debris into viable building components become common practice?

CHYBIK + KRISTOF + TEAM + JAN STOLEK + BREATHE.EARTH.COLLECTIVE + LESY CESKE REPUBLIKY + HRADEC KRALOVE, CZ = **FORESTRY IN THE FOREST**

Year: 2017
Type: offices
Size: 12,000 m²
Investment: EUR 19,000,000
Status: competition (1ˢᵗ prize), ongoing

Branching i

o the forest

to immerse i

n atmosphere

shared experience

which unites us.

Welcome to m

nner woodland.

It might be hard to find me amidst the dense woodlands in which I reside. In fact, one will need to embed themselves within the landscape before finding my entrance. My angular lattice-structured façade will be framed using a wood similar to the different types of trees that surround me. My green roof canopy will resemble the forest floor below. It's not so much that I want to conceal myself but rather that I want to immerse myself in the setting. I'm set to become the largest wooden structure in the Czech Republic upon my completion.

As the new administrative centre of the Czech Forestry Commission in Hradec Králové, it's only normal that I should practice what I preach. My expansive 12,000 m² of office space will branch out into the landscape in my immediate vicinity.

My architect's concept for my integrated development won out over 40 other submissions entered by major international firms. The architect's proposal was one of the only to fulfil the vision of a future-oriented environment that could feel more like an open public institution conducive to its context rather than a standard office block. The jury was also impressed by the proposed use of material. I'm set to be constructed in a wood frame with cladding painted in muted greens and large glass exposures that maintain a close connection to the world outside.

Employees working in one of my many tentacular wings will be surrounded by trees and have access to nature through my courtyards. They will be constantly reminded of what they're fighting for but also operate in a healthier environment. They'll never be too far from saplings pushing up within the gaps that form between my structure. Sensory gardens representing different types of forest will occupy each semi-enclosed outdoor space. Why can't an office be situated deep within the forest, especially one dedicated to ecology? I'm as much about the indoor spaces I encapsulate as the outdoor spaces my footprint delineates.

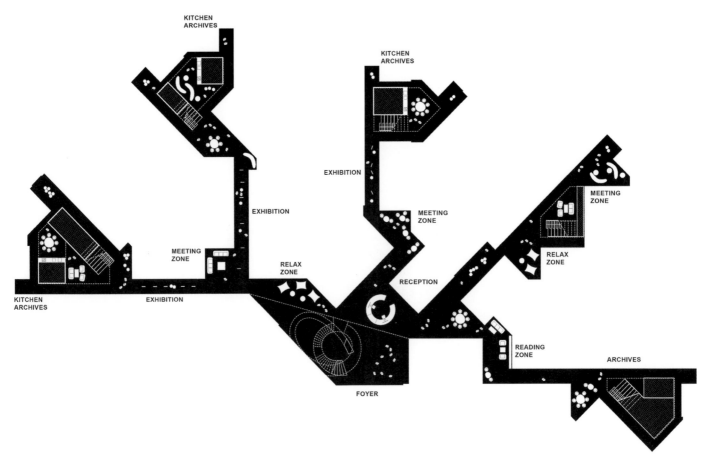

KITCHEN
ARCHIVES

KITCHEN
ARCHIVES

EXHIBITION

EXHIBITION

MEETING
ZONE

MEETING
ZONE

MEETING
ZONE

KITCHEN
ARCHIVES

RELAX
ZONE

RELAX
ZONE

EXHIBITION

RECEPTION

READING
ZONE

ARCHIVES

FOYER

Shared spaces functional diagram

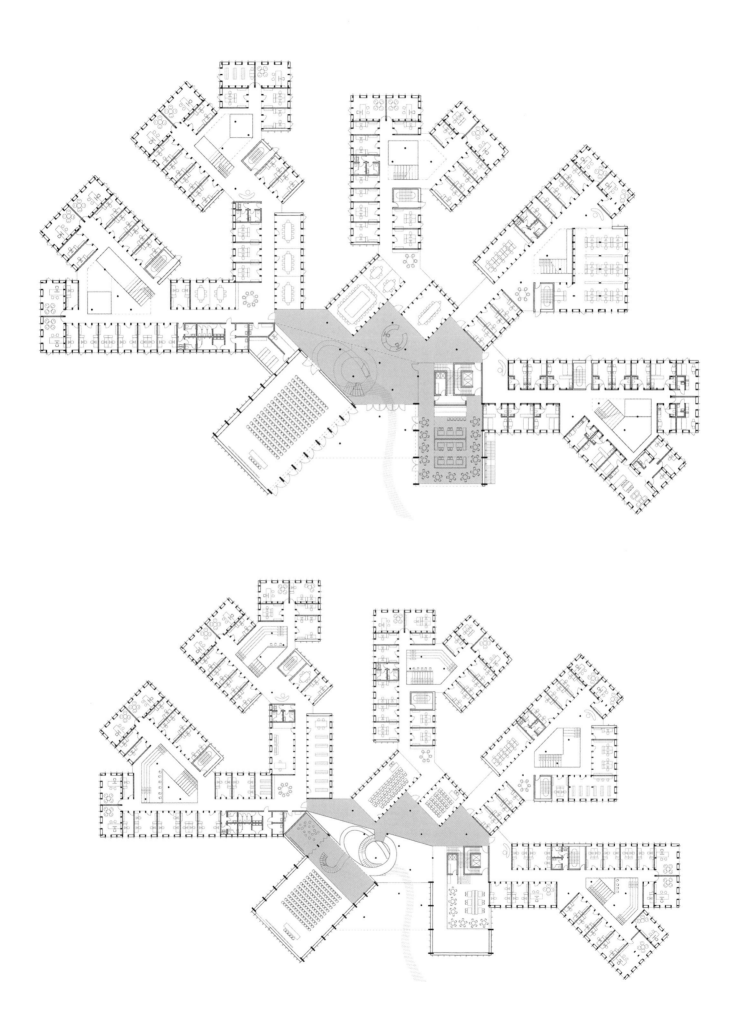

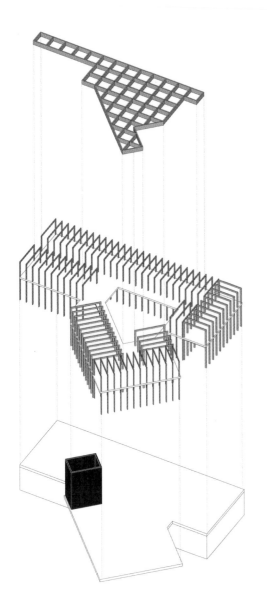

Spatially rigid structure grid

Frame structure of the offices

Reinforcing core and concrete base

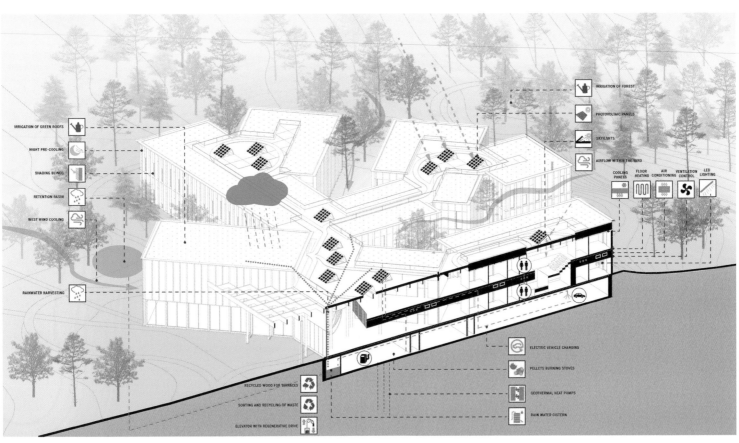

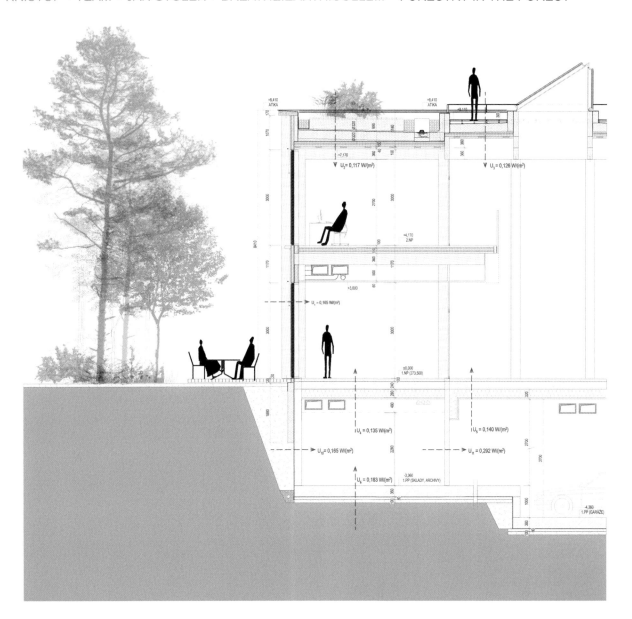

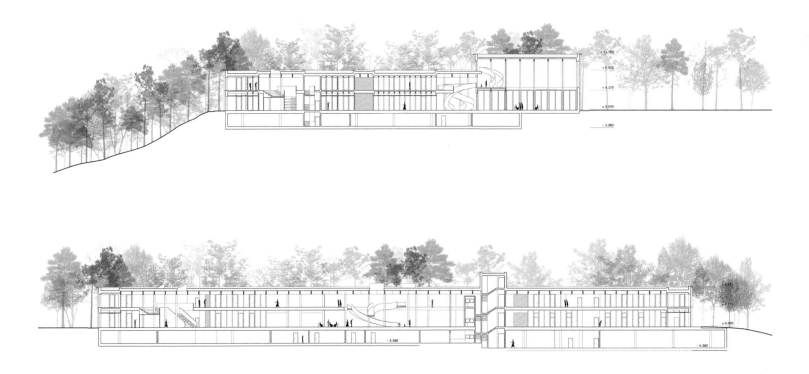

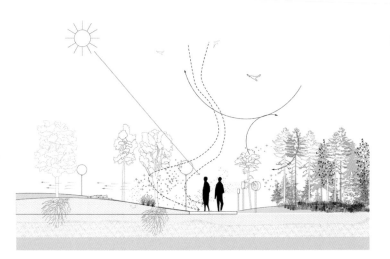

Park Forest

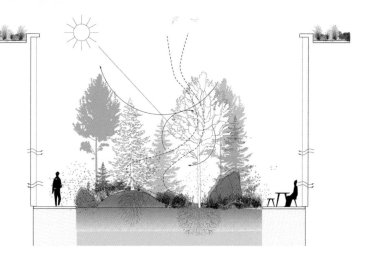

Mountain Forest

Spruce Forest

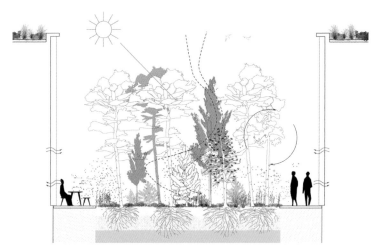

Sandy Forest

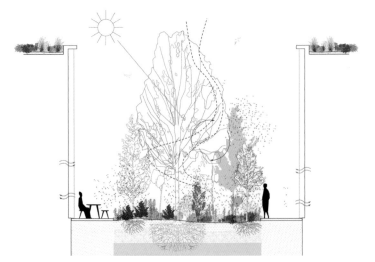

Ashfort Forest

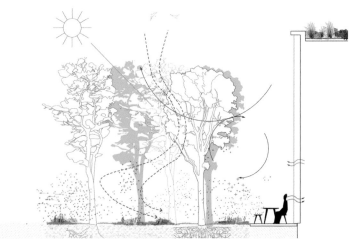

Riparian Forest

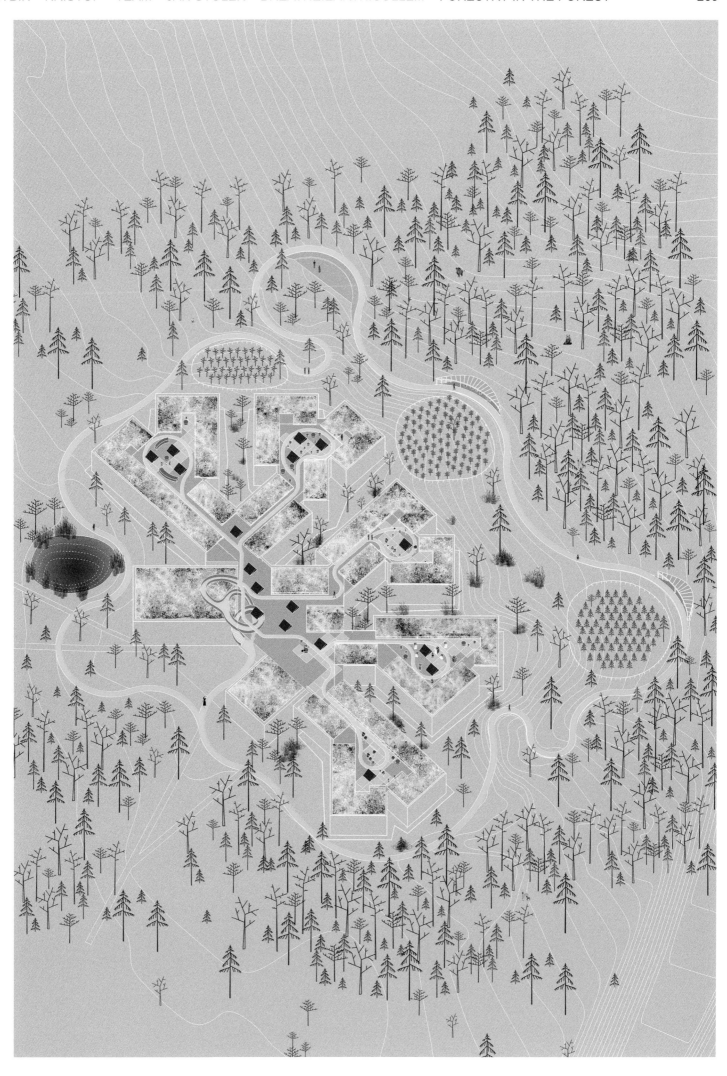

CHYBIK + KRISTOF + TEAM = SELF-INITIATED TRANSFORMATIONS

The ability to develop a concept free of the demands of a specific client can seem like a dream scenario. One is able to achieve their own vision and solve a problem that few want to tackle. However, taking on such a project can prove to be a great challenge and requires a significant amount of self-motivation, time, passion and the willingness to wear multiple hats. Engaging in such initiatives, architects need to push beyond their traditional remit and adopt the roles of community advocate, historian and producer – garnering financial support from both public and private entities. They end up developing and enacting entirely new methodical strategies. Taking on what developers or policy makers might not is a chance for practitioners to leave their mark on the built environment, flex their creative muscles and improve social and cultural conditions. Identifying who the client and stakeholders are helps inform the requirements of a project and establishes a dialogue between all the parties. As demonstrated in the revitalisation of Zvonařka Bus Station in Brno, self-initiated endeavors can take years to achieve but ultimately produce results that embody the qualities of intentionality, social responsibility and consciousness. In this chapter of Crafting Character, Chybik + Kristof substantiates its skill and willingness to self-initiate regardless of scale and complexity.

 CHYBIK + KRISTOF + TEAM + CSAD BRNO HOLDING + BRNO, CZ = ZVONARKA BUS STATION

Year: 2017–2020
Type: civic, transformation, bus station
Size: 10,000 m^2
Investment: EUR 5,000,000
Status: completed

My renewed

character

in the new

melight.

I had waited

ong enough

ÚSTŘ

a new chapte

My raw concrete-and-steel canopy was first designed in the 1980s by prominent structural designer Radúz Russ, and constructed in 1985 to reflect the Brutalist/High-tech style that was popular throughout central and eastern Europe at that time. Since my opening more than three decades ago, I've operated consistently as one of Brno's main transportation hubs but as of the early 2000s, I fell prey to decay. Locals saw me as a reminder of an architectural style closely linked to previous political systems and so didn't see value in my rehabilitation. Though quick fixes were introduced to ensure I could still operate, my true essence was gradually disregarded. Like with other examples of the incredibly expressive and experimental architectural style – including the Hotel Praha and Transgas buildings – I could have easily been demolished and replaced by now but my architects stepped in right on time. The firm did everything in its power to keep me alive and bring my former glory.

Based nearby, the architects observed how neglected I was and set out to bring me back to my former glory. They took it upon themselves to prove that my seemingly unsalvageable structure could be restored and still serve a purpose. For them, it wasn't just about preserving my brutalist imprint, one of the last examples of that movement in the country, but also ensuring that I could answer contemporary demands: thousands of passengers traveling on hundreds of regional, national and international bus routes.

My architects developed and presented their elementary study and redesign proposal to the station's private owners and garnered public appeal by publishing the plans on social media. The scheme promptly drew significant media attention. This spawned a fervent four-year-long discussion between private stakeholders and public authorities, which ultimately helped the owners to secure financial backing from the European Commission.

CHK and their partners spent another four years carefully analysing and refurbishing the structure without causing any damage or disruption to transportation. Special lighting fixtures designed for this project that could fit into the building seamlessly and create the illusion that its floating, will also illuminate the space underneath.

Today, my Brutalist overhang – Brno's largest covered public space – hovers above the flurry of activity that occurs below. I have no walls but accommodate an indoor waiting area encapsulated within one side of my span. Natural light filters through and casts dramatic shadows on the relief of my defining roof. Commuters and travelers alike can identify me and my function from a significant distance. Am I a beacon for Brno? Only time will tell.

What CHK proved by taking each of these steps is that architecture can be as much about design as the mitigation of social, political, cultural, historical and environmental factors that activate a place in time. This negotiation is an inherent obligation when shaping the built environments we use every day.

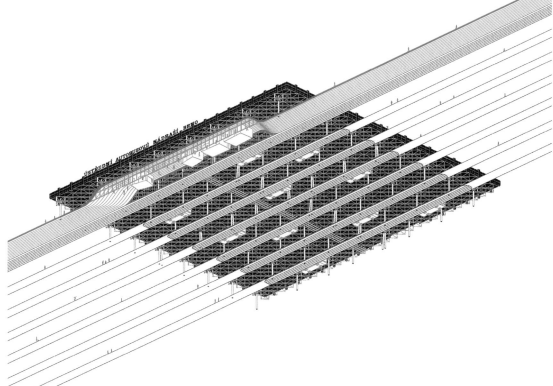

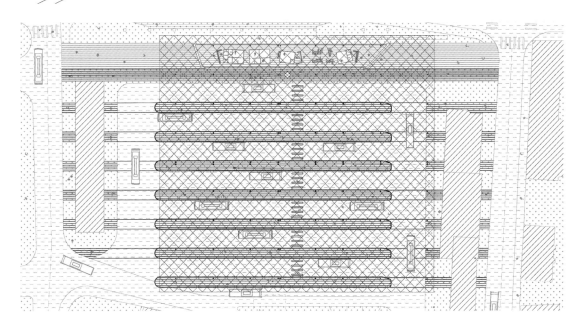

Drawing form the original project documentation, 1984

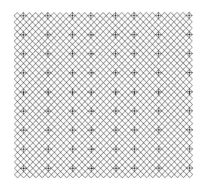

Renewed structure of the terminal

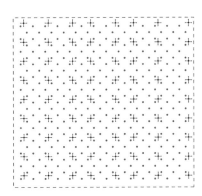

Lighting fixture placement

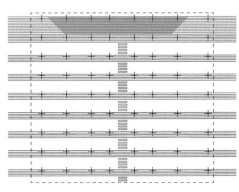

New organisation of the bus station

The architects envisioned the concept of permanently scaffolding my canopy with a clever wavepattern matrix of steel beam, an entirely contemporary and perhaps anachronistic scheme but that would make the historical element stand out.

CHK, general conductor PS Brno sro, engineering firm K4 and other partners spent another 4 years carefully introducing the new support structure without causing any damage or disruption to transportation. As one section of the armature was introduced, an old column was removed. The architects removed any non-essential structures that were added over the years.

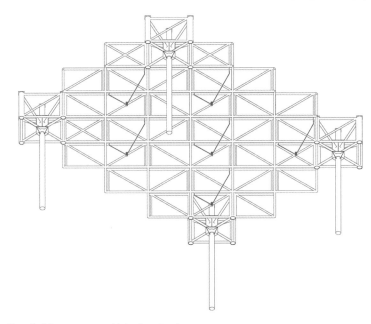

New lighting composed into the structure

CHYBIK + KRISTOF + ADRIAN MADLENER = CONVERSATION

Ondřej Chybík and Michal Krištof

Stara Boleslav Primary School, winning competition proposal, 2023

Ondřej Chybík and Michal Krištof

Ondřej Chybík and Michal Krištof view architecture as a dialogue that arises in both public and private sectors. As demonstrated in their diverse output, examined in this book, they're particularly interested in exploring where these two contexts intersect. From its offices in Prague, Brno and Bratislava, the duo's firm Chybik + Kristof (CHK) coalesces around a wide range of considerations. From addressing site specificities and environmental factors to ensuring a locale's history is respected while bringing it up to contemporary standards, it develops all-encompassing designs that fufill complex briefs.

Regardless of if the firm is working in the cultural, commercial, civic, residential, public space, transportation, hospitality or research sphere, CHK looks to ease generational and societal differences with the ultimate goal of creating spaces that are better connected to their surroundings, stand the test of time and are more inclusive.

As both principals often emphasise, dealing with underlying issues typically involves fostering meaningful engagement; directly confronting the main challenges of a project to generate impactful solutions. This strategy is achieved by using a diverse array of tools and techniques evident in their treatment of projects from the Lahofer Winery to the Zvonařka Central Bus Terminal. Enacting such bold programmatic shifts often centres on a strong aesthetic sensibility.

CHK's dynamic approach sets it apart. The firm has secured hundreds of commissions over the past decade with many garnering it top accolades. These include the 2017 Grand Prix of Architects; 2019 Design Vanguard award; the 2022 nomination for EU Prize for Contemporary Architecture – Mies van der Rohe Award; amongst an endless list of prestigious prizes and competitions.

By offering complementary insight into their respective and shared histories; what drives their process; how they're planning for the future, Chybík and Krištof emerge as the conclusive characters of the Crafting Character book.

Prague Airport extension, study, 2020

ODA - Tirana's Center of Fairs and Exhibitions and mixed-use development, competition proposal, 2023

How did you decide to pursue architecture as a potential career?

ONDŘEJ CHYBÍK: I grew up building and learning how things fit together. Both my parents were educated as engineers and so it made sense to follow in their footsteps but not do exactly what they did. I studied architecture and urban design at the Brno University of Technology, in my hometown, before my other studies at Graz University of Technology in Austria and the Federal Institute of Technology (ETH) in Zurich, Switzerland. After that, I worked for the Viennese architectural studio PPAG, which specialises in educational buildings and social housing. This experience significantly influenced how I view architecture and the role it should play in our society.

MICHAL KRIŠTOF: Unlike Ondřej's clear path to architecture, I came to the profession by chance. I was born in a small Slovakian village called Klastor pod Znievom. My parents worked in entirely different fields. I chose architecture as a potential direction when considering what to study. I quickly developed an affinity for the discipline and the rest is history. I attended the University of Technology Brno and did a 1-year Erasmus exchange at Catholic University Leuven, Campus Sint-Lucas Ghent in Belgium. Then I worked at Bjarke Ingels Group in Copenhagen, Denmark. These were incredibly formative experiences. I've been a guest critic and lecturer at schools like the Academy of Fine Arts in Bratislava, Politecnico di Milano, Italy and Cornell University in Ithaca, New York.

What inspired you to establish an independent practice together rather than working separately at established firms, where most architects end up spending years rising up hierarchies before actually developing their own ideas.

KRIŠTOF: Ondřej and I were in the same class in architecture school and to be honest, we weren't really that close! Maybe it was rivalry, maybe it was admiration, somehow through our mutual respect and ambition, we decided to start practicing together after we came back from abroad. We found out that it was better to collaborate than to compete. We were both very interested in what we could create together and how we could combine our experience and skills. The collaboration arose out of curiosity.

CHYBÍK: It all began with a competition to design a private gallery on a Finnish island. We ultimately lost because we were up against 400 other firms but what the process proved is that we were capable of putting our egos aside and collaborating. Winning our second competition – a housing project situated along the Danube river in Bratislava allowed us to establish the firm, build our first functional team and pay our employees fair wages.

Seeing that our partnership was both creatively fruitful and economically viable, we started to dream without restraint.

Talk about how you founded the firm based on the idea of not doing what everyone else was already doing.

CHYBÍK: We founded the studio in 2010 right as the financial crisis landed in Central Europe. It was hard to figure out how we would get our first non-competition-based commissions. Our preliminary task was to survive, especially in Brno where every second doorbell is an architecture firm; small, medium or large. Thrown into the scene, our aim was to get visibility and gain credibility all while sticking to our goals of remaining autonomous and not diluting our core creative vision of site-specific revitalisation, useful adaptability and sensible innovation. This book explores how we've acted upon many of these values by highlighting key characteristics of some of our most important projects.

KRIŠTOF: One area where we made a stand was in introducing new concepts of sustainability in both master planning and architecture on environmental, economical and social levels. Valuing the importance of public spaces, we were able to win, for example, our first big project: a master plan redevelopment of a former brownfield site in Prague – Waltrovka and Modřanský Cukrovar (otherwise called Sugar Factory) into residential districts. At the moment, looking back to our beginnings, we are happy that we decided to stay in the Czech Republic and Slovakia. Both markets are still in need of important projects. There was a lot of potential for us in beginning our studio here. We were able to have a bigger impact than say a firm just getting started in Belgium or Denmark. In the past, most Czech architects that became well-known did so by practising in places like London. Our idea was always to be firmly rooted in our home countries while also developing projects around the world.

How did you gain exposure over time?

KRIŠTOF: Designing for competitions – at first those that were open calls and eventually ones in which we were invited to participate – brought us early acclaim in the architecture community but it was through our public relations strategy – having projects featured in different online and print magazines – that we were able to communicate our philosophy to a wider audience. On the one hand, we were able to share what we think architecture is about and what it can achieve to the general public; and on the other hand, made sure our projects were getting seen. It was less about promoting the commercial aspect of producing more and more buildings but actually creating better designs. We've always wanted to make structures that better meet our client's needs but also address complex socio-economic conditions and even incite dialogue within different communities. We've always been open to sharing our ideas and that has made us more attractive to potential clients: individuals, companies and governmental agencies.

How do you complement each other as co-principals?

CHYBÍK: There's a lot of trust and shared curiosity. It takes effort to develop a strong concept. Being able to value each of our ideas, even if they seem outlandish, is important when putting our heads together. There's an openness to experiment but also an underlying level of mutual respect when it comes to critiquing each other. Regardless of how out-of-left-field they may be, every idea that's brought to the table is evaluated with equal rigour. This approach allows us to quickly distil what's key in a brief and move forward without hesitation.

KRIŠTOF: Architecture students are still educated to be individuals, who are able to do everything on their own. In reality, architecture is a collaborative profession and success can only really be achieved through cooperation. We realised early on that we didn't need to do everything on our own and that we could delegate, divide and manage. Our ambition was always to develop large-scale projects, not just single-family homes or interiors. We knew that we needed to create a strong team to be able to take on such endeavours. The firm grew steadily by bringing on the best available talents, many of which were our friends and former students. This same spirit informs how we approach our clients – ensuring they play an integral role in the process – but also the way we work closely with other external experts from around the world.

Through the various projects we've explored in this book, it's clear that you operate with a unique approach. Further explain how you develop projects on a daily basis.

KRIŠTOF: The firm has expanded step by step since we started in 2010. Because our team has become so big, we've structured our office with a simple hierarchy of team leaders and project managers that oversee different commissions at any given time. Ondřej and I don't have to be involved in every meeting or deal with small details. We as principals, don't spend all of our time dealing with administrative tasks and it frees us up to do what we like most and that is the designing. We are still deeply involved in every project.

As mentioned before, it's about being open to different lines of inquiry and interests but also knowing how to coalesce these sources of inspiration into viable concepts that address different requirements and needs, and not just those of the main client either.

We use different methods, but we usually offer them around five well-developed design options that are nuanced yet completely different. Presenting them with floor plans, sections, 3D renderings, full architecture presentation and physical models of each allows us to collectively pick and choose qualities we like and combine them in final designs that can sometimes look very different to what was originally put on the table.

What's most attractive to our client is our ability to choose a clear direction but expand on it as much as possible. We feel that this is a responsible way to answer almost every aspect of the complex briefs we receive. It's also an effective way of easing them into accepting innovations or unconventional solutions that might otherwise seem too radical.

Slovak pavilion at Prague Quadrennial, completed, 2019

Construction of Apartment Houses in Nusle mixed redevelopement, together with CMC, ongoing, 2017–2024, Prague

Aesthetics seem to be a big part of what you do. Talk more about how this consideration comes into play?

CHYBÍK: For us, including strong visual elements is as important as a project's programme. Often, all of these considerations come together and complement each other. We're rarely interested in following a set house style but more in championing what's unusual about a given site and its environment. Like with Lahofer Winery we approach the look and feel of every design by addressing specific requirements. Across the board, however, simplicity is key. Finding new ways to boldly express a building's purpose or the initial concept we developed; either in its façade, interior layout, the materials it incorporates or the details we introduce, is deeply important to us. Gallery of Furniture is a strong example of that. Our intention is always to be emphatically transparent. Even if clarity is essential, we're still interested in celebrating all of the complexities of a project. It's a balancing act. We're always creating spaces that are slightly different from your standard white box.

How has architecture evolved since you began practising?

CHYBÍK: The role of an architect has completely changed in the past decade. It's no longer just about designing buildings based on your own aesthetic but rather operating as a facilitator; wearing more than one hat in trying to find all-encompassing solutions. An urban master plan is as important as the singular structures it might contain. The notion of placemaking, taking into account different needs and perspectives, is now a vital part of the discipline. Vltava

Philharmonic Hall and Mendel Square are demonstrative of this shift. For us, it's about taking your own initiative; an approach we took to re-develop Zvonařka Central Bus Terminal. If you see problems in the spaces you frequent often, you don't need to wait for a commission that might never materialise. You can harness your knowledge to imagine improvements and even make small but impactful interventions by yourself. This is how we started out and in some cases, how we continue to operate.

Looking to the future, what would be your dream project?

KRIŠTOF: It was essential for our studio to start in our local market, to get experience, references and to get strong position here first. After that it was always our vision to work internationally, first across Europe then across the globe. This entire journey is a dream project itself.

CHYBÍK: Complexity is applicable everywhere but each market or scene is slightly different in what it's looking toward. While hybrid timber structures might be popular in France and Germany at the moment, densification is important elsewhere. We believe that our versatile approach can be applied almost anywhere. The proposal to adapt 1633 Broadway in New York is a great example of this vision. Though conceived for entirely different end-users, the design of an iconic winery in one place and the development of a multi-use affordable housing campus in another deal with the same fundamental issues that this book has uncovered.

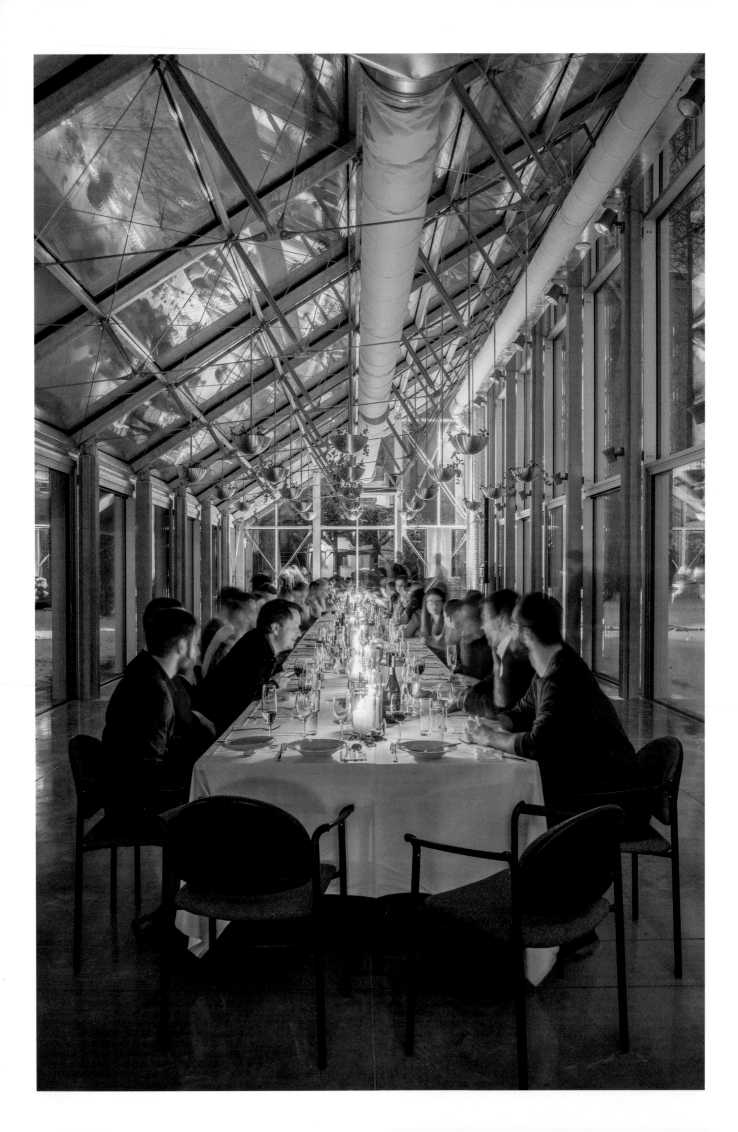

CHYBIK + KRISTOF = **TEAM**

Dominika Adamcová + Hanin Al-Gibury + Sara Al-Wahaishi + Adam Ambrus + Jana Andrašíková + Denisa Annová + Aian Giménez Azurmendi + Pavel Bánovský + Martina Barborjaková + Mária Bažíková + David Erik Bernátek + Dorian Beydon + Kristýna Blažíčková + Frida Block + Martyna Anna Bobińska + Martina Bognerová + Zuzana Bojdová + Laura Bonfiglioli + Štěpánka Bucharová + Kamila Buchholz + Peter Chaban + Roman Chervonnyy + Denis Cheryn + Lenka Chládková + Martin Chudíček + Ondřej Chybík + Victor Cojocaru + Gabrielle Coudert + Adrián Bonet Cózar + Magdalena Maria Czopka + Gabriela Čermáková + Benjamin Daniels + Martin Decký + Laura Druktenyte + Marcin Dryjer + Lan Duongová + Lucia Ďurčová + Petra Dušková + Mária Dvorská + Burcu Eyupoglu + Emanuele Faggion + Petra Figlovská + Jitka Floriánová + Kryštof Foltýn + Marek Frait + Andrea Fűlőpová + Tomáš Gebhardt + Filip Gladiš + Giulia Gori + Luis Gutierrez + Lukáš Habrovec + Alan Hackl + Antonín Hadrava + Meike Hagemann + Hanna Hajda + Antonín Hampl + Pavel Haniš + Jan Havlíček + Martin Holý + Pavel Hrůza + Martin Adrian Iglesias + Isabela Ignacio de Moura + Thomas Julian Ivanov + Fleta Jakupi + Ondřej Jelínek + Robert Jelínek + Klára Jeníková + Adam Jung + Magdaléna Juřicová + Louai Kaakani + Michael Kalábek + Oliver Kažimír + Tomáš Kecek + Jakub Klíma + Jakub Klimeš + Michal Klimeš + Andrej Kocian + Ján Kohút + Richard Kokeš + Justyna Konopacka + Martin Kopecký + Anastasiia Korchagina + Natália Korpášová + Martin Kos + Maroš Kostelanský + Lenka Kostíková + Vojtěch Kouřil + Jakub Kozák + Petra Krajčová + David Král + Ivo Kratochvíl + Kristína Krchová + Michal Krištof + Martin Křivánek + Šárka Kubínová + Marianna Kubová + Klára Kuklínková + Kristína Kujanová + Martin Kulaga + Nikola Kumstátová + Matej Kurajda + Tereza Kvapilová + Lukáš Kvasnica + Petra Lálová + Ilya Lebedev + Jan Lebl + Viktor Makara + Miroslav Malý + Gabriela Marková + Dávid Medzihorský + Lucie Mejsnarová + Veronika Mesíková + Ondrej Mičuda + Peter Mihaľák + Jiří Mika + Veronika Mikulková + Luca Minotti + Maroš Mitro + Zdeněk Modlitba + Alex Montolio + Francisco Javier Gomariz Moreno + Eliška Morysková + Iva Mrázková + Ondřej Mundl + Lenka Musilová + Katerina Musilová + Albert Novák + Petr Novák + Dominika Novobilská + Karina Pak + Marta Palazzo + Ondrej Palenčar + Veronika Pálková + Tereza Panáková + Markéta Pavlunová + Zuzana Pelikánová + Jiří Peterka + Daniela Pisingerová + Hana Pleskačová + Dávid Podešva + Antonín Pokorný + Iva Potůčková + Petr Preininger + Tereza Přidalová + Jiří Příhoda + Andrea Rampasová + Jiří Richter + Lucija Ritoša + Michal Romanec + Vanesa Rybárová + Laila Sabsabiová + Radek Sátora + Mario Sebastian + Urszula Sędziak + Antonio Seghini + Jozef Seman + Anna Serysheva + Vadim Shaptala + Clément Schwab + Johana Simkovičová + Dagmar Sitařová + Ela Siwiec + Lucie Skořepová + Michal Sluka + Stanislav Smolík + Lukáš Sochor + Ingrid Spáčilová + Małgorzata Stachoń + Ivo Stejskal + Jan Stolek + Eva Straková + Marek Svoboda + Jan Šefl + Luděk Šimoník + Vladimír Šobich + Marie Šotkovská + Lenka Špirudová + Jitka Šťastná + Matej Štrba + Vojtěch Štýbnar + Ondřej Švancara + Zoltán Takács + Piotr Talárek + Alexandra Taraboanta + Alexandra Timpau + Sophia Tligui + Brittany Trilford + Lukáš Vajda + Jiří Vala + Kateřina Vaňatková + Jakub Vašička + Vít Vávra + Ondřej Venclík + Gabriela Vera Soto + Jan Vetchý + Thao Vi Nguyenová + Kateřina Vítková + Magdaléna Vojteková + Gabriela Voláková + Lenka Vořechovská + Vanda Výbohová + Tomáš Wojtek + Tomáš Wolf + Denisa Zalud + Zuzana Záthurecká + Denisa Zatloukalová + Paulína Závacká + Přemysl Zhoř + Stanislava Zubová + Eliška Žáková + Martin Žatečka + Ondřej Žvak.

CHYBIK + KRISTOF + NOOR AL QAYEM =
AFTERWORD

This book comes at a time of unprecedented change in spatial design. Or does it? It seems that everyone has been citing 'unprecedented change' in just about every industry for the past 2 years. Everyone believes themselves to be living in a time that is constantly changing, and for good reason: it is. In spatial design this poses a unique challenge: architecture requires a stable foundation. How can we design for a world that is fated to forever be shifting? How may we embrace that instability and excitement? What may be relevant one moment may not be the very next. That is why it is so important to consider context. More than just consider, however, good design is fundamentally embedded in contextual awareness; it is relational in essence. Having considered the various relationships between the people, the histories, the site, the surroundings, relational design aims to be adaptable, long-lasting and inclusive.

It is in this space that Chybik + Kristof have positioned its studio. Its designs consist of an all-encompassing sensitivity to the relationships which surround a project, carefully balanced between past, present and future considerations. Unafraid of experimentation and playfulness, the team is willing and able to push the boundaries, question the status quo and not take themselves too seriously. When first describing the studio, François-Luc Giraldeau (the book's commissioning and managing editor) told me told me, 'they're just really cool, aren't they?' Even with this monograph, the principals and collaborators were up for anything; experimenting with design, tone, format, language… everything.

Chybik + Kristof's projects are the characters in this title (drama, if you will), and they have told their stories in their own voices. In doing so, they have rendered themselves as inextricable participants in their shared contexts. Speaking of oneself necessarily means speaking of one's context; making oneself legible as a kind of negative space through the definition of one's surroundings. This makes for a holistic understanding of what architecture is and how it can operate in a world of constant change. This understanding is one that posits that architecture is not created in a vacuum, but is fundamentally defined by its background, history, surroundings, origins, margins, impacts, intentions, visitors, builders, thinkers. This is the fundamental ethos of relationality; an intentional decentralisation.

Relationality can be applied to any creative endeavour, including this book. It is defined by the people who wrote, designed, contributed to it, and by the people who will read it. It is defined by the books and objects it will sit next to on shelves, tables, desks, counters, floors, in shops, homes and offices. A book has staying power; an immortalising effect. As does architecture. However, it is a mistake to believe that any creative output, including books and buildings, are at all static in nature. The meanings will constantly be shifting, through the relationships that develop over their lifespan. The telltale sign of any creative endeavour that has stood the test of time is that it is flexible and agile enough to shift along with the changing times and attitudes. Gone are the days of short-sighted design and one-track minds. Our present challenge is to live in the moment, while planning for the future, all while having fun with it. Chybik + Kristof, in its designs, have offered up methodologies for how this may manifest in the spatial design field. Only time will tell.

CHYBIK + KRISTOF = ACKNOWLEDGEMENTS

We would like to express our gratitude to everyone who has contributed to making this book possible.

First and foremost, we would like to thank our team and colleagues for their unwavering dedication and creativity over the years. Your hard work has been instrumental in bringing our projects invoking character to life. We could not have done it without you.

We would also like to extend a special thanks to our colleagues working on this book – Ela Siwiec, Brittany Trilford for initiating and shapping the project and Urszula Sedziak for working tirelessly to ensure its success. Thank you for your dedication and hard work.

To the team at Frame Publishers, especially François-Luc Giraldeau and Noor Al Qayem, for being incredible partners in creating our studio's first monograph. Their openness to experimentation and support throughout the process made it a pleasure to collaborate together.

To Adrian Madlener for his unwavering patience throughout this endeavor. His exceptional writing has gracefully given our projects a voice, seamlessly bringing them to life within the pages of this book. It was a pleasure to read your words.

To Aaron Betsky, we extend our sincere appreciation for our insightful discussions about architecture and his time spent visiting the Czech Republic. Your essay has added a layer of depth to this book, and we are thankful for your contribution.

To TIMES NEW REALISM + ExLovers studio, particularly Lukáš Kijonka and Zuzana Kubikova, for our long-lasting collaboration and for giving our studio, and especially this book, a visual edge.

We would also like to extend our appreciation to the photographers who have skillfully documented our projects. A special mention to Alexandra Timpau, Laurian Ghinitoiu, Pavel Barták and Jesús Granada for their work. Your photographs have wonderfully captured the essence of our endeavours, adding visual appeal to our documentation.

We extend our sincere appreciation to all of our collaborators and partners, particularly those whose projects are featured in this book. Your support and contributions have been invaluable in helping us create meaningful and impactful architecture.

Finally, we wish to extend our profound gratitude to all our clients, commissioners, and partners throughout the years for entrusting us with their confidence in our creative instincts and architectural expertise. Your collaboration and support have been priceless in shaping the vision and mission of our studio, and we eagerly anticipate the continuation of our partnership in the years ahead.

Lastly, we would like to convey our deepest appreciation to our exceptional wives, Zuzana and Anna, for their unwavering support. We are truly thankful for your constant inspiration, the fortitude you provide us, and your dedication to both our personal and professional journeys. We are forever appreciative.

Once again, we extend our heartfelt thanks to everyone who has contributed to our work over the years, and, by extension, to this book. Your involvement has been immeasurable, and we are enthusiastic about the prospects that the future holds.

Ondřej Chybík and Michal Krištof

CHYBIK + KRISTOF + TEAM = IMAGE CREDITS

All images copyright to Chybik + Kristof Architects [CHK] unless otherwise noted.

PHOTOGRAPHY

Simon Oberhofer
6

Radek Brunecky
7

Alexandra Timpau
8, 18–19, 20–21, 24–25, 30–31, 32–33, 36, 37, 38, 39, 48–49, 56–57, 58–59, 62–63, 64–65, 66, 67, 142–143, 144–145, 146–147, 149, 150, 180–181, 182–183, 188, 189, 190, 230, 273, 274–275, 276–277, 278–279, 280–281, 282, 292

Lukaš Pelech
9, 75, 76–77, 78–79, 80–81, 82–83, 84–85, 86,

Laurian Ghinitoiu
16–17, 22–23, 26–27, 28–29, 36, 37, 38, 47, 50–51, 52–53, 54–55, 67, 217, 218–219, 220–221, 222–223, 224–225, 226–227, 228–229, 231

Pavel Barták
39, 60–61, 69, 188, 231, 241, 294

Lukáš Prokeš
102

Mecanoo
135

Marek Jehlička
140–141, 150

Filip Urban
148, 169

Jesús Granada
177, 184–185, 186–187, 188, 189

Julius Filip
178–179

Tomáš Hejzar
240

Simona Modrá
288

VISUALISATIONS

Plomp
110–111, 112–113, 114–115, 125, 126–127, 128–129, 132–133

Mecanoo
130–131

Monolot
155, 158–159, 160–161, 162–163, 164–165, 166–167, 169, 290

Igor Brozyna
199, 200–201, 202–203, 204–205

Vivid-Vision
239, 242–243, 244–245, 246–247, 248

MISS3
253, 254–255, 256–257

FlyingArchitecture
258–259

Bucharest Studio
290

ILLUSTRATIONS

Alexey Klyuykov

191, 192, 210, 211, 212, 213, 249, 250, 251

Laura Emilija Druktenyte
103, 104, 105

DRAWINGS

Breathe Earth Collective

268

Mecanoo
136

ARCHIVAL MATERIALS

249 – Photo from the archive of the Office of the Municipal District of Prague 12

169 – Photos from the archive of the Město Jihlava

102 – Photos from archive of the city of Ústí nad Orlicí – Lukáš Prokeš

134 – Images courtesy IPR Praha

107 – Image: New York City.jpg by Gerd Eichmann is licensed under Creative Commons Attribution-Share Alike 4.0 International. Source: Wikimedia Commons

284 – Drawing from the original project documentation, 1984